BATTLE FOR BATAAN

Col. Richard C. Mallonée, top left; Col. Nemeseo Catalan, top right; Gen. Luis Villa-Real, bottom left; Gen. Douglas MacArthur, bottom right.

BATTLE FOR BATAAN

An Eyewitness Account

from the diary of
Richard C. Mallonée

edited by Richard C. Mallonée II

★

PRESIDIO

This edition printed 1997

Copyright © 1980 by Presidio Press

Published by Presidio Press
505 B San Marin Drive, Suite 300
Novato, CA 94945-1340

Library of Congress Cataloging-in-Publication Data

Mallonée, Richard C
  The naked flagpole.
    1. World War, 1939–1945—Campaigns—Philippine Islands. 2. World War, 1939–1945—Personal narratives, American. 3. Mallonée, Richard C. 4. Philippine Islands—History—Japanese occupation, 1942–1945. I. Mallonée. Richard C., 1923–   II. Title.
D767.4.M34   940.54'26   80-15538
ISBN 0-89141-619-6 (paperback)
ISBN 0-89141-094-5 (hardcover)

Printed in the United States of America

Contents

	Foreword	vii
	Preface	ix
1	The Gathering Storm	3
2	Four Months and a Day	19
3	The Death March	143
4	Guests of the Emperor	159

Maps

Lingayen Gulf Landings	37
Withdrawal in the North	39
Holding the Road to Bataan	59
Through Layac Junction	65
Situation in Bataan	89

Foreword

The World War II Battle for Bataan was one of the most important battles of the war in the Pacific. That was because it delayed the Japanese advance long enough for America to arm Australia and prevent the Japanese from taking it, thus saving the superb continent as the base we needed for our movement back north to regain the Philippines and subsequently force Japan to its knees. Without Australia our task would have been almost impossible—it was tough enough as it was. The Japanese commander in the Philippines was relieved of his command for failing to take the Philippines in a timely manner, illustrating how Japan felt about the importance of securing Bataan promptly.

Now that more than fifty years have passed since the surrender of Bataan, the history books have relegated it to a casual mention, if it is mentioned at all. Most school boys know more about the Alamo than about Bataan, yet Bataan involved more than ten times as many people, and lasted four months and a day.

Even though the British had far more field guns, and far more food and ammunition for the defense of Singapore, and even though they were engaged after the Bataan campaign had started, they capitulated before Bataan. Colonel Richard Mallonée and his compatriots were always a little bitter about that, for they had had the hope that fighter aircraft could hedge-hop from Australia to Singapore, and then to Bataan, to replace the fighters destroyed at Clark Field (not realizing that Roosevelt had no plans to do so, even if it had been possible).

Colonel Mallonée was liberated at Mukden, Manchuria, by elements of the Russian Army who had cut in under the Japanese Kwantung army by crossing the Gobi Desert. The Russians took the one million man Kwantung army into captivity in Siberia, and the majority of them never returned.

This is the only account of the Battle of Bataan, the Death March, and the subsequent prison camp life based on a day-to-day diary written by one of those who suffered through it. It was used by Louis Morton when he wrote the official army account of the fall of the Philippines. There have been several sensationalized accounts of the Bataan Death March, but nowhere else is the suffering of the prison camp delineated. It is fitting that it is being reissued and made available to America as another account of the gallantry Americans have always illustrated when under adverse military situations.

Richard C. Mallonée, Ph.D.
Seattle, Washington

Preface

When the radio news of Pearl Harbor reached the Philippines, we in USAFFE—that very imposing title for such an unimposing military force, the United States Armed Forces in the Far East—knew that we were next.

We received our orders from headquarters, North Luzon Force, and in chaos and bewilderment moved to our beach defense positions on Lingayen Gulf. The North Luzon Force was completely incapable of carrying out its mission of preventing the Japanese from landing on Luzon shores.

The regimental and higher commanders and staff officers in the force were, with a few exceptions, American regular army officers or career officers of the Philippine Scouts, highly trained and dedicated. We knew the odds against us and knew what to expect. So we had a rather sardonic belly chuckle when we read the exhortation written probably by some rear-area junior staff officer, to the effect that we were to hold our positions at all costs, to die falling forward toward the enemy.

When we got our teeth kicked in and were driven off the beaches, not too stupendous a military effort for the Japanese, our orders were changed to more realistic ones. We were to fight delaying actions on a series of defensive positions, south across the rice paddies of central Luzon, withdrawing into Bataan Peninsula where defensive positions of great strength had been prepared.

In my opinion the withdrawal of the Luzon army from the beaches to Bataan is an epic worthy of a place in history alongside many other examples of "lost cause" actions. I am proud to have been a member of that force and to have contributed my small part to its success. I definitely consider its action was a success. The delay imposed upon the enemy at the beach and during the withdrawal, the fact that the Philippine army withdrew to Bataan maintaining its cohesion, the fact that it forced the enemy to bring his best troops in large number to reduce Bataan—all these things threw the Japanese march to the south off its calculated time schedule.

In my opinion it saved Australia and New Zealand by allowing time to reinforce those nations, and it saved India by diverting troops, shipping, and material intended for an operation there.

If in dealing with the defense of the beaches and the withdrawal into Bataan I appear overcritical, or if I have created the impression of fault finding, or have seemed to be throwing blame upon the Philippine army, I can only say that such was not my intention. I constantly tried to improve the tools with which I had to function in battle. If I had been in command I would have attempted to do the job in a different, and I think a better, way. The fact that my regiment had many faults and weaknesses does not alter the fact that it did a fine job in which I took great pride.

The route of withdrawal of the column I was with passed through Angeles, just a short kilometer or so from Fort Stotsenburg. Nostalgia made me detour and visit the post, although I knew that the garrison had been withdrawn and the fort abandoned. I wish that I had not made that detour.

I entered the deserted post past the Storm King, over whose summit the gathering clouds foretold the coming of the typhoon rains, and I stopped for a moment in front of 9 Wint

Avenue. No. 9 Wint—that set of quarters where I had lived so
happily with my family during the country-club era of the
middle twenties.

The bombing of nearby Clark Field had taken some toll of
Stotsenburg. The roof of No. 9 had collapsed. The front
screen door hung on one hinge. The jungle was coming swiftly
down from the nearby Zambales Mountains to reclaim its own.
Weeds were three and four feet high. Crawlers and climbers
were tearing at the screens and pulling down the *mediagues*—
the *swali* sunshades.

I drove on to the artillery parade ground, the parade of the
24th Field Artillery, Philippine Scouts. It had been a beautiful
parade. The houses and barracks surrounding it, all with their
meticulously manicured lawns, were lined with fire and flame
trees that were gorgeously beautiful with their crimson glory
at the proper season. Now it was different. There were chuck-
holes in the roads. Weeds were waist high, climbers choking
the trees.

Memory carried me back to the retreat parades, with their
pomp and formality and color. The commander of troops
would call us to the "present." Each officer's saber would
flash up in the sunlight and then down to the salute position.
The retreat cannon would be fired and the band would play
the national anthem. The flag would come fluttering down,
lowered slowly from pole top into the waiting arms of the corporal of the guard, who was meticulously careful that not one
fold should touch the ground.

I turned and looked at that flagpole. Many years later, the
picture of that naked flagpole was still etched across my
vision. It should not have been such a shock. I was a regular
army officer. I knew what to expect. I knew the post had been
abandoned. I knew what was about to happen when I left. But
the sight of the pole without the flag that had fluttered there
for almost forty years was more than I could bear. It was a
symbol of the things taking place, and, even more, of the
things to come.

As I left the post through the hospital entrance, I turned for one last look at that naked flagpole. I was filled with a mixture of emotions: frustration, irritation, despair, bitterness, white-hot anger. But the principal taste in my mouth was from the dregs of shame; the knife wound of humiliation in my heart.

My friends through the years have laughed at me. After all, it was just a flagpole. They have laughed at me for being so sentimental. Yes, I am sentimental. I have a love of country, a pride of country. I openly admit of my patriotism. I was brought up that way. I was trained that way. I honestly believe that the great majority of my fellow citizens feel the same way, but in our present generation we cloud that feeling behind a mask of indifference. Laughter greets the avowed patriot.

That naked flagpole, then and now, symbolized our inadequacy, our futility, our ineffectiveness, our impotence, our inability to hold back the advances of what we thought to be a second-class power. It symbolized the rubbing of our military noses in the dirt.

And why? In 1941 we were a powerful and rich nation. We had had ten pretty tough years, but we had recovered from the economic debacle of the depression. We raised, trained, and equipped many divisions of citizen soldiers, divisions that participated with great efficiency in the 1941 Louisiana maneuvers, divisions that were to demonstrate their combat readiness within a short time after Corregidor fell. What would have happened had we had a few of those divisions in the Philippines?

We had sent tons upon tons of Lend Lease across the Atlantic. We gave fifty destroyers to England. What would have happened had those destroyers been in Philippine waters?

What had we done for our Filipino friends? We sent them one reduced-strength regiment of antiaircraft artillery with practically obsolete guns, a few lightly armored vehicles that didn't deserve the dignity of the name tank, a few guns, and a few airplanes. We sent some personnel as individuals, not as organized units—senior officers like myself and junior youngsters just out of college ROTC.

I know all the arguments of my Anglophile friends. Russia was bled white. England was tottering. We could not fight two major wars in two opposite directions. Germany would conquer the world while we were engaged in a second-class war. There is much merit in these arguments. But I will never change my opinion that just a little—oh, so very little—would have been necessary *before* Pearl Harbor to have made the handwriting on the wall so clear to the Japanese government that Pearl Harbor would never have taken place.

As I took my last look at the naked flagpole and turned away, it was with the feeling that it was as a virgin being abandoned, betrayed, left to be violated and befouled by the conqueror—and all so needlessly. There should never have been a naked flagpole. It could have been prevented. It should have been prevented!

BATTLE FOR BATAAN

1

The Gathering Storm

On September 10, 1941, I was in command of the 12th Field Artillery, 2nd Division, during the second Third Army maneuvers in Louisiana. I had a fine outfit that was building an enviable reputation. My operations sergeant brought me a grapevine report that I was under orders for the Philippines. At 9 A.M. the next day I received a red-ball letter directing me to sail from San Francisco on October 4. By noon I had turned over my command and was on my way.

After settling my family in La Jolla, where they were to remain during my tour of duty in the Philippines, I sailed on the appointed day on the army transport *Willard Holbrook*, formerly the *President Taft*, which was accompanied by the transport *Tasker Bliss*. There were seventeen field artillery officers on the two ships, and to my surprise I was the senior passenger on the *Holbrook*.

We reached Honolulu October 9 and left before dawn under convoy of the cruiser *Chester*. The ships were blacked out at night; this seemed a strange precaution since we were not at war.

We landed at Manila after dark October 23, and I went on to Fort Stotsenburg the same evening.

The next day we reported. Officers who were ordered "for duty" with the field artillery, Philippine Department, were assigned to the regular Scout Artillery. The rest of us went to USAFFE (United States Armed Forces in the Far East) duty with the Philippine army in the service of the United States.

The officers assigned to Scout units rubbed it into us. They were to stay at Stotsenburg in comfortable quarters with servants, an officers' club, a cold storage plant stocked with American meat, and all the comforts of post life. More important, they were to command old-line units, well equipped and well trained, with noncommissioned officers of many years' service. We, on the other hand, were to go into the field to newly constructed bamboo- and *nipa*-shack camps lacking electricity, plumbing, and other conveniences. Our units were newly organized, partially trained or untrained, undisciplined, officered primarily by short experience, partially trained reservists, and equipped with makeshift material. I believed we would have some compensations, possibly in increased rank, because of the importance of the responsibilities given us.

We were given a talk on post regulations and customs by Lieutenant Colonel Galbraith. He emphasized the appearance of officers at all times, and especially the use of "whites." I was rather surprised, as I had thought that with the women gone home the bachelor post would be more or less under field conditions.

Dinty Moore* and I were temporarily assigned space in one of the vacant sets of quarters. By some freak of coincidence, it was the same set I had occupied so happily with my family in 1927. Ghosts of happy memories surrounded me—and made me rather miserable.

---

*Lieutenant Colonel A. P. Moore.—Ed.

After several days of inactivity, we were assembled for an orientation lecture by the post commander, Brig. Gen. Edward P. King, Jr., commanding general, North Luzon Force. The general stressed several points: that there was no such thing as racial superiority; that any superiority evidenced must be that of demonstrated leadership; that the Filipinos were a proud and sensitive race and many of their reactions had their root in real or fancied racial slights; that throughout history the Filipino soldier had demonstrated personal bravery and individual fighting ability, even against superior arms; that our job was to train and weld that individual fighting ability into organized fighting teams. The general cautioned us to be meticulous in our relations with the Filipinos. He warned us not to judge them by our standards, emphasizing that they were not immoral but amoral; not lazy but physically incapable of prolonged exertion; not dishonest but lacking in understanding of our code; not liars unless the need was essential to escape embarrassment, disgrace, or loss of pride.

I had served in the Philippines before, from 1926 to 1929, as a battery commander in the 24th Field Artillery at Stotsenburg and for about two years as the assistant G-3 (operations) at department headquarters in Manila. During the latter period, while General MacArthur was the department commander, I was acting G-3 for a considerable time. I had visited and studied nearly every vital defense area on Luzon, Cebu, Iloilo, and Mindanao. I had thus been thrown into contact with many elements of the Filipino people, from the rice-farming *tao* to the political intelligentsia. I had studied them all with a lively interest. After my return to the United States, I continued to study their history and kept myself reasonably well abreast of current developments.

As a result, I agreed in the main with General King's analysis of the Filipinos. But I found it difficult to concur with his views on their potential. I doubted the ability of the leaders to weld the mass into a fighting machine. I could not visualize the

Filipinos' simplicity, physical softness, lack of vigor, absence of individualism, fear of the supernatural, and unwillingness to seek or assume responsibility as combining to make tough, intelligent, alert, aggressive fighting men. I had grave doubts that the Filipino intelligentsia, from which the officer corps had to come, was capable of leading the masses into battle in modern warfare.

But my judgment was based on conditions as I knew them fifteen years previously. I could see in a few days that great strides had been made in many fields since then. Possibly, military leadership had developed. I hoped so. I remembered also that the opinion held by General King was expressed to me, unqualifiedly, by General MacArthur during a talk I had with him in Washington in 1936 or 1937 when he came home to be married.

I was interested in just what the Philippine army was and was to be. From various sources I gathered the following information.

During the previous four years forces of various size had been called annually for five and a half months of military training, with the result that between 100,000 and 120,000 men were trained, classed as reservists, and assigned to specific divisions. The Philippines were divided into ten military districts, with one division in each district. Seven of these military districts, and thus seven divisions, were on Luzon; the others, in the Visayas. As men were trained, additional reserve divisions were to be formed until by 1946, independence year, about forty divisions would exist.

The divisions were constituted along the lines of the American triangular divisions but with some modifications I did not care for. Total strength was about 8,000 men, a reduction from about 15,000. There were three infantry regiments of three battalions each but with a total of only 1,800 men to a regiment. My principal concern was the reduction of field artillery firepower. Instead of the American organization of three battalions of 105-mm. howitzers and one battalion of 155-mm. howitzers, totaling fifty-six guns, the Filipino organization had only one regiment of three two-battery battalions with a total of twenty-four guns. There was no medium artillery (155-mm. howitzers) in the division at all, nor any 105-mm. howitzers. The armament was the 2.95-in. mountain pack howitzer and the British 75-mm. gun. The howitzers were the same ones we had fifteen years before, and they were obsolete and worn out even then. Nor did I have a very high regard for the British 75 Model 1916. I was told that before January 1 the Philippine army would receive "many" 105-mm. howitzers and 75-mm. pack howitzers from the States. Somehow I doubted it.

None of the divisions were actually in existence. Several regiments had been called and were at training areas. Most of the others had cadres in training—officers and key noncommissioned officers. In the case of the field artillery, the cadres of all ten regiments were assembled at Stotsenburg's Camp Del Pilar in September and had been under intensive training since then. The division commanders, their staffs, and the regimental commanders—as many as were in the Islands and available— had been attending a school at Baguio. Rumor had it that the bulk of the divisions were to be called up the latter part of November. The deciding factor seemed to be completion of construction at the training camps.

Of the seven divisions to be constituted on Luzon, five were to be in the North Luzon Force and two in the South Luzon Force. The training camps were sited in the potential defense areas. The North Luzon Force had the 11th and 21st Divisions abreast in the Lingayen Gulf area, the 91st covering Balete Pass and the approach from Aparri from the vicinity of Cabanatuan, the 71st in reserve at Camp O'Donnel, and the 31st covering the area west of the Zambales and Subic Bay from San Marcelino. In the south the 41st and 51st covered Batangas and Tayabas.

Philippine army officers came from several sources; former

Scout and Constabulary officers formed the bulk of the senior command and staff. The junior officers were, in small part, from the recently constituted Military Academy, commanded by my old friend, "Smoke" Segundo. They were proudly referred to as regulars. I did not see that they differed materially from the reservists who formed most of the officer corps, being of similar age, experience, training, and education. Our group went daily to Camp Del Pilar to observe the training of the field artillery cadres—the young officers, NCOs, and specialists —who were to form the nucleus of our regiments.

I was not very happy about the status or method of training. First, the opportunity for practical instruction was very limited, with only a small amount of material available. More limiting was the fact that not one round of service ammunition or subcaliber training ammunition was available for practice firing. The instructors were principally young American reserve officers, young Filipino officers, and Scout NCOs. They were similar in age, education, and experience to the young officers I left behind in the 12th Field Artillery: fine, bright, intelligent, interested young men, but with little training or experience.

As a result of limited training facilities and inexperienced instructors, instruction was largely theoretical, out of the book. The students were keen, enthusiastic, and bright as new whips. They knew the "book" by heart and were parrot-perfect in their answers. But they had only a faint idea of the practical application of book knowledge, and they did not appreciate that the examples in the texts were guides only, seldom actually encountered.

I attended one field exercise involving the placing of a battalion in position but occupying only one battery position. The exercise demonstrated a complete lack of basic understanding of the tactical principles involved, and the technical mechanics, so glibly demonstrated on the sand table the day before, were ignored. It was glaringly evident that the students failed to see any connection between the academic problem in the text and the practical problem on the terrain.

I was assigned as "senior instructor" of the 21st Field Artillery Regiment, 21st Division. Moore received a similar assignment to the 41st Field Artillery, 41st Division. In the other eight divisions an American officer received command of the artillery regiment, a distinction I did not understand. Later I learned the reason. The 21st and 41st Divisions were to be commanded and officered entirely by Filipinos; so were the other divisions, eventually, as capable leaders emerged, before the Islands' independence in 1946. But the need for American guidance was still evident, hence the instructors. I was not at all happy about my assignment; I had had my belly full of instruction work—responsibility without authority.

The regimental commander of the 21st was Lt. Col. Nemisio Catalan, whom I remembered as a young lieutenant in the 24th Field Artillery in 1927. He had retired as a captain for physical reasons, but later he connected with the Philippine army and served in several junior staff capacities. He told me he had never commanded any military unit, even a battery. A graduate of the Los Banos Agriculture College before getting his commission in the Scouts, he was used at Stotsenburg principally for post beautification and police work. His troop duty was mainly with service battery. He was sent by the Philippine army to Command and General Staff School and seemed somewhat disgruntled that he was not selected as a division chief of staff. I had doubts about his qualifications, but I was wrong.

The regimental executive was Capt. Luis A. Villa-Real, a regular officer of four or five years' service. He struck me as a most intelligent, highly educated, well-qualified young officer. He had attended Culver Military Academy, was a graduate of the Fort Sill Field Artillery School, and went through the 1940 Louisiana maneuvers with the 77th Field Artillery Battalion. With Colonel Catalan at school in Baguio, Villa-Real assumed many functions of command, among them the assignment of the regimental staff and battalion and the battery commanders.

The battalion commanders were a shock to me. Valdez could not have been over twenty-six or twenty-seven, and Mercado and Acosta looked about twenty-three. Valdez had five years of active service, during which he was a battery commander for one training period of five and a half months. Acosta and Mercado both were 1940 graduates of the Philippine Military Academy, but neither had even commanded a battery.

There was no motor transport for the field artillery regiments. We were to receive a command car and two trucks from some of the regular units. As the regimental commander would have priority on the car, leaving me flat-footed, I decided to buy a car. It was a 1938 Buick sedan, in excellent condition, on sale by a Fort Stotsenburg sergeant.

I was assigned some young American reserve officers as assistants: 1st Lts. George Reed, Carl J. Savoie, and Roderick Hendry, and 2nd Lt. Thomas R. Harrison. I lost Reed to the self-propelled artillery (SPMs) before the war. The three remaining, all recent college graduates and all detailed from the Scout Battalion, had among them a total of thirty-seven months of active service. But they did a magnificent job. Savoie received a Distinguished Service Cross and a Silver Star; Harrison got a Silver Star; and Hendry was recommended for a Distinguished Service Cross, but he was turned down after the war, when Bataan had faded into limbo.

I had assumed there would be written instructions clarifying and defining my duties and responsibilities as "senior instructor," but none appeared. So on November 19 I reported to General King and asked if written orders spelling out my status and authority could be expected.

His answer was illuminating. "Absolutely not. That would be too dangerous. This instructor business is dynamite. You must be the epitome of tact. Be careful. Under no circumstances issue any orders. You must get your objectives by suggestion and recommendation. But you are directly responsible for the success or failure of the regiment. If you cannot get full cooperation from Catalan, write me a confidential letter or come in and see me. Remember, I am holding you directly responsible for the efficient functioning of that regiment."

I had a caved-in feeling. There was so much to be done in the regiment and I was eager to wade in. The prospect of going around the barn instead of using direct methods was most distasteful.

Shortly after 6 A.M. November 20, Thanksgiving Day, I left Fort Stotsenburg with my American officers and our baggage for the induction center at Bayambang, where the bulk of the reservists who were to form our regiment were to be received, examined medically, clothed, equipped, and sworn into service. We stopped at Del Pilar to collect the cadre of advance detail: battery commanders, first sergeants, supply sergeants, clerks, and cooks. I picked up Colonel Catalan in my car. We arrived at Bayambang about noon. Our Thanksgiving dinner there, a slimy chicken stew, will be long remembered.

In theory, the induction center had in storage all the equipment for the regiment other than motor vehicles, field guns, and fire-control gear. In reality, I found shortages of clothing and personal equipment and, in many cases, a complete lack of many essential items of organizational equipment.

Catalan and the induction officer were certain that the reservists would start arriving Saturday and be ready for the acceptance oath by 9 A.M. on the 24th as scheduled. Accordingly, I approved plans to have civilian motor transport ready to move at that time.

The regimental enlisted strength was 1,004. Deducting the cadre, there were 830 men to report. They did indeed start coming in Saturday. The medical exam was a bottleneck; but the medics worked late that night and almost all Sunday night, and by 9 A.M. Monday every man who had reported had been examined, clothed, put in ranks with his battery, and was ready for the oath, which I administered. There were exactly

500 of the required 830, but there was a procedure to receive and forward the late arrivals.

The men were mainly Pangasanans, but included were numbers of Illocanos, Pampangans, and a few Bontocs. Most had only a feeble command of English. It was discouraging to realize that instruction in English would have to be translated two or three times before it reached all the men. It was equally discouraging to learn that about eighty percent of them had been trained as infantry during their five-and-a-half-month training period and had no artillery experience at all.

As soon as the induction procedure was over, we loaded out in fourteen large open buses for the trip to our training camp at Sta. Ignacia. Loading was an experience the like of which I hope I never have to suffer again. Each bus could seat fifty or sixty men, with equipment and other impedimenta stowed on top, tied on behind, wedged underneath, and held on the men's laps. There was no vestige of order or discipline in loading. All the men got aboard first and then had to be pulled off, almost by main force, to load the equipment. Then, as each man would load one item, he would get back in the bus, settle himself comfortably, produce food from somewhere, and start eating. It took almost three hours to do the loading—a job that should have taken about twenty minutes.

The American officers had forwarded our baggage and mess equipment from Stotsenburg directly to Sta. Ignacia. Hendry and Reed had gone with the truck, taking Bernado Montoye, my house cook. Hendry, who was mess officer, had gone over the camp with Bernado and arranged for our baggage to be in our *bahays* (huts), the mess gear to be unpacked, and a meal to be waiting for us at 1:30 P.M. Monday.

Upon arrival, we found everything piled in one *bahay* exactly as Hendry had left it, no mess, and no Bernado. Sometime later Bernado drifted in. "Ah—sir. . . ." He had been through a horrible experience. The first night he had slept alone. There had been an evil spirit, a ghost, who had wanted his soul. He had been forced to fight all night. In the morning he had been obliged to take refuge in the barrio, where he had found a kind companion.

I asked him why he had not returned in the daytime with the men Hendry had hired, unpacked the mess furniture, and set up the mess. "But—ah, sir—these people are Pangasinan and I am Pampango. They are very bloodthirsty and I was in fear of my life."

The thing was so silly as to be amusing were it not that I had the job of welding the Filipino—and Bernado was a typical example—into a tough, aggressive fighting man.

Our training camp was on the edge of the barrio of Nambalan, about a kilometer south of Sta. Ignacia proper, which was some thirty kilometers north of Tarlac on Route 13, a secondary road to Lingayen Gulf. The camp's *nipa*, bamboo, and wooden buildings were nowhere near completion. The site was astride the main dirt-and-gravel road, and heavy clouds of dust from the road's considerable traffic covered everything. My *nipa* shack was beside a carabao wallow, where deposits of green slime harbored myriads of large flies and droves of mosquitos. The officers' latrines were close to the officers' mess shack, which had no stove or other equipment. Of course, there was no electricity.

Although a well had been dug, there was no pump or storage tank. We hauled water from Camiling, twelve kilometers away, in my car and Reed's until we received the promised command car and two trucks. After that the trucks—Dodge four-by-fours —seldom stopped, one hauling water, the other rations and other purchases.

The men were kept busy keeping the area free of litter from the construction, knocking down rice paddy walls, filling in the carabao wallow, digging latrines, making walks, leveling drill grounds—the thousand and one things necessary before drill could begin in earnest. We had no guns or vehicles. There was a mass of administrative work, all of which had to be done in longhand.

I was able to devote a little time to military work. Catalan and I made a reconnaissance of our assigned beach defense area from Lingayen to Sual Bay, and I prepared a terrain monograph to use as a basis for tactical problems for the battalion officers pending the arrival of enough material to start technical instruction.

As yet there was no division instructor. I made several trips to division headquarters trying to establish a training program or at least some sort of division instruction plan. The division commander, Col. Mateo Capinpin,* was buried in a maze of administration. The assistant G-3, Tuason, was the only one of the staff who seemed to have given a thought to coordination of training, and he was snowed under with other people's work.

Another week passed and something was accomplished. We built bamboo guns and held standing gun drill. Daily physical exercises, rifle instruction, sighting and aiming drills, push-pull exercises, telephone procedure, as well as disciplinary close-order drill, started to make the regiment look like a military unit. Each battalion instructor prepared a tactical exercise based on my terrain monograph and walked through it with the battalion officers.

Maj. Stanley B. Bonner joined me, having just arrived from the States. He was a temporary major (regular captain), a specialist in communication, and a graduate of the Signal Corps School at Monmouth and the Field Artillery School communications course. I was delighted to have him, especially as he told me, after a few days of working with the communication sections, that their training at Del Pilar was a little more than perfunctory and we had no men able to operate either the SCR 161 radio or a telephone switchboard. He started an intensive program both for assigned men and for additional students and installed simple field communication telephone nets.

---

*Soon to be promoted to brigadier general.—Ed.

Wednesday afternoon I went to Stotsenburg on a triple mission: to call on General Wainwright, who had relieved General King as commanding general, North Luzon Force; to have a conference with the force G-3; and to get a week's supply of food for the mess.

I missed General Wainwright, who left the post on an inspection trip to San Marcelino. I had a talk with his new chief of staff, Col. William Maher, whom I had known casually at the Field Artillery School at Fort Sill, Oklahoma, some years before. I wanted clarification of my status in the event of war and was surprised to find there was no doubt in his mind that the instructors would remain in their capacity if war came. I could not visualize such a situation: a commander upon the battlefield with an adviser, instructor, inspector—call him what you want—camped on his tail, checking his every thought and action, interfering with the estimate of the situation, and interjecting his own personality into deliberations and decisions. It sounded unworkable.

I also thought it damned unfair to both instructor and regimental commander—especially to the latter, who is responsible for the success or failure of the unit in battle. I said so, rather heatedly, to Maher, who replied he didn't agree with me, that if it was unfair to anyone it was unfair to the instructor, for he was the one, not the CO, who would be held responsible for the unit. If all went well, the instructor would hover silently in the background while the CO got the plaudits. But if the going got tough, the instructor was expected to step in and take the command through his "leadership qualities, using great tact." God, how I was getting sick of those words.

The discussion continued, Maher obviously getting impatient with what he considered my obstinacy, until he closed the interview with these words: "Mallonée, if war comes I can tell you in so many words just what General Wainwright will expect of you. You will have to command that regiment whether you get any order to do it or not. The buck is yours and if that outfit fails you fail. The general is getting damned sick of the entire instructor mess and is seriously considering placing the instructors actually under command of the Filipino commander. But don't worry about it. It looks like a mess now, but it won't be if war comes. You won't have any trouble. I know these Filipino officers well. I served as a Scout officer in the old days. I know Catalan. There isn't one of them who won't be tickled pink to have the responsibility for decision taken out of his hands—they will be more than willing, they will be anxious." Thus I was again told you can't do the job your way, but you must get the job done or it is your neck.

On my way back I stopped at division infantry. Col. Ray M. O'Day had joined as division instructor. From my contact with him I believed the artillery would be left severely alone, which would be fine. I could go ahead with my own training ideas—provided war didn't interfere.

The Stotsenburg people seemed easy and looked for trouble, if any, in the spring. Radio announcer Don Bell had the same idea—that the Tojo cabinet was a stopgap which would give way to either a war or a peace-at-any-price cabinet in the spring. But if I were the Japanese general charged with invading the Philippines, I would not want to do so in the spring with the rainy season coming up, but immediately.

On December 6 I lost Lieutenant Reed, who was transferred to the new self-propelled artillery being formed at Stotsenburg. Also, I received twenty of our 75-mm. guns and the next day the other four. Sixteen were equipped for high-speed trailing, but eight still had the wooden wheels of the horse-drawn days. At last we had something to train on, although as yet we had received only fifteen panoramic sights, fifteen quadrants, fifteen fuse setters, some field glasses, and enough fire control equipment to give one aiming circle and one battery commander's telescope to each battalion. We had 200 rounds of service ammunition per gun and 100 rounds of rifle ammunition per man.

At 7 A.M. the next day (December 8 in the Orient) I switched on the radio and heard the news of the attack on Pearl Harbor. The gathering storm had burst.

2

Four Months
and a Day

At midmorning on December 8, Colonel Catalan and I were ordered to report to division headquarters, where we found the other regimental commanders and instructors assembled. About 10:30 A.M. we received our first official news of war.

I was disgusted and alarmed over the soviet that developed. No one and everyone was in charge. All talked at once, all argued trivia. The situation was simple. North Luzon Force radio had ordered divisions to concentrate within four hours' marching distance of their assigned defense areas and await orders. We were already so concentrated. But because we had no trucks, the artillery had to await not only orders but transportation.

Some officers argued that we should continue training until an invasion was reported imminent; others, that since orders would be only a matter of hours we should get packed up and be on the roadside ready to go. The commander of the 21st Division, Col. Mateo Capinpin, vacillated between the two viewpoints.

I was vitally interested in two matters: trucks to haul our guns to the beach and where the guns would be placed when

19

we got there. I finally got Capinpin's ear and a staff officer was dispatched to force headquarters to inquire about trucks. As for battle positions, I was astonished to find they had been selected by a reconnaissance party of which Villa-Real was a member. Many years earlier the department G-3 section had maintained a complete file showing the positions for light and medium artillery, with fields of fire, as well as water depths, channels, and other data indicating potential landing points. I felt sure this information had been maintained and updated, and that our positions could best be selected from it. But I was unable to get Capinpin or Lieutenant Colonel O'Day, the division instructor, to evince the slightest interest in it. So after twenty years of continuing and unhurried reconnaissance and study, we were to occupy positions selected during a forty-eight-hour trip over 120 kilometers of front by a major of Constabulary and a reserve captain of limited experience.

We returned to Sta. Ignacia shortly before noon. After a sketchy lunch we heard the hum of airplane motors and then, for the first time in the war, machine-gun fire. Several Japanese planes were working over a lone American P-40, which almost immediately burst into flames and fell like a rock. We saw the pilot bail out and float slowly to earth. Soon a native boy dashed in on a pony and said the aviator needed help. There was no motor road to the location, about four kilometers away. I sent a doctor and litter bearers with the boy. They returned about two hours later with the pilot, but he died en route to the hospital.

About 4 P.M. trucks and buses loaded with infantry began to stream through our camp, and I assumed the force order for movement had been given. Shortly afterward a division staff officer stopped, en route forward, but had no orders or information for the artillery and knew nothing except that division CP was moving to Bugallon on Lingayen Gulf. O'Day stopped by later. He had no orders for the artillery either but told us the division was going into battle positions. He also said that force headquarters had emphasized this was to be a last-ditch defense, the beach was to be held at all cost, and there would be no withdrawal. He advised us to sit tight and await orders. About 5 P.M. we received word from a Manila transportation company that five large trucks were en route to us, with nineteen more to follow.

Another division staff officer, Tuason, passed through. He said there was no evidence that an enemy landing expedition was anywhere near Luzon. He was also certain that no buses would be available for our personnel until the next morning, when the division infantry movement would be completed. Consequently, I recommended that despite the danger of being bombed during daylight we use the dark hours to load, if the trucks did arrive, and move out the next day. Orders were given to break out the kitchens, feed the men, and then let them get some rest.

No sooner had this been done than I heard some noise of confusion and found that despite Tuason's assurances the buses *had* arrived. Catalan had decided to send the regimental and battalion headquarters' batteries forward and, since the buses were there, I agreed even though we still had no orders to move and it would be a night march without lights. Shortly afterward the five big trucks arrived, followed several hours later by eleven smaller ones.

Loading was as chaotic as it had been at Bayambang. The buses and trucks were arriving piecemeal, and we did not know how many there would actually be. Thus, it was impossible to assign a certain number of vehicles to each battalion; as the buses arrived we assigned them, based upon capacity, to each battalion in turn. As each bus moved into place, all men in its vicinity swarmed over it and fought each other for seats, then had to be forced out to load equipment. The officers had great difficulty getting the men to obey; Hendry, the mildest-mannered and most even-tempered of the American officers, had to use a flailing piece of bamboo on one occasion. I deplored the means, but it got effective results.

We assigned the five big trucks to the 1st Battalion, since

these had pintles and could easily trail the guns. The other eleven were small one-and-a-half-ton or three-quarter-ton vehicles, commercial types lacking pintles, tie chains, or even ropes. We had to unload the five large vehicles so a gun could be placed in each of their beds in addition to the one that each trailed. Guns were lashed behind the small trucks with plaited straw, belts, *bahucca*, or anything else resembling rope. The trails had to be suspended by a loose tie beneath the truck; otherwise, the gun muzzles would have been only about six inches from the ground.

I discovered one battalion commander had not loaded his ammunition because he lacked space. When his trucks were unloaded to make room, I noted that every officer's oversized bedroll and clothing roll had been loaded, as well as such un-authorized impedimenta as suitcases, truck lockers, guitars, and boxes of every size and description.

With the big trucks taking ten guns, and the small ones and our two Dodges thirteen more, one gun had to be left behind when the leading battalion finally moved out at 11 P.M., four hours after loading began. The last battalion left about 2 A.M. Catalan and I followed the last element in my car.

The ties on the small trucks broke many times during the night, guns went into the ditch, trucks broke down and had to be repaired, trucks crawled up on guns—but all guns arrived undamaged on the beach shortly before 5 A.M. December 9. We sent back for the gun that had been left behind, and it, too, was in position before dawn.

At Bugallon we found Capinpin raging like a caged lion. There were about twenty more trucks parked in the open, figuratively, on the doorstep of his CP. He was trying to get them moved, but his bellowing efforts accomplished nothing except to move the civilian drivers to less conspicuous sleeping places. I suggested that his staff could accomplish this while he got some rest, but from the profane incoherency of his re-marks I gathered his staff had evaporated to well-concealed places of rest.

I curled up on the front seat of my car to take a short rest myself. I had no more than arranged myself when Lieutenant Savoie arrived with the news that the 3rd Battalion had arrived at its rendezvous but was unable to find the staff officer placed there by Villa-Real. The battalion was standing on the road with no idea where to go, no cover within a kilometer, and enemy bombers expected. I snatched Villa-Real out of bed and sent him back with Savoie. It developed that the 3rd Battalion staff officer had become tired and was lying down in a convenient *nipa* shack.

After this, I unloaded, got my maps together, and started out for a look at the battalion areas. When Catalan and I made our reconnaissance of the area, I had refreshed my memory of the terrain. There were two methods of placing the artillery at the beach. The first was to put the guns 1,500 to 2,000 yards behind the water's edge and direct fire from observation posts on the beach. This required both efficient telephone or radio communication and efficient officers as observers. We had barely enough telephone wire to string one line from the regimental CP to each battalion; our communication personnel were totally incompetent; and none of our officers had ever fired a round of field artillery ammunition in service practice.

The second method was to place the guns at the water's edge where the crews could point their pieces directly at the target. This simple method, like aiming a shotgun, would permit us to use the communication net for tactical control, and if communication broke down, the local unit would still be able to function.

The trouble with this was that the beach presented little opportunity for camouflage; hostile aircraft would have no difficulty spotting the guns. It was impossible to protect the guns and crews by digging in—before an effective depth could be reached water would be encountered. Protection would have to be built up, using sandbags and logs, which would increase the ease of their being located from the air. We could expect that any landing would be preceded by air and naval bombardment, and it was possible that before enemy boats ever got within range most of our guns would be out of action; certainly our personnel losses would be heavy.

I had elected the beach defense with guns at the water's edge when Catalan and I made our reconnaissance, based upon the condition of our regiment then. I saw no reason to alter that decision and Catalan agreed. I visited the battalion positions for the first time on the morning of December 9. Villa-Real had done a good job, and with two exceptions the guns were in the positions he selected.

I reached the 1st Battalion area, on the extreme right in the vicinity of Binmaley, shortly after dawn. This battalion had a field of fire from well to the east of Dagupan (our division boundary) and extending west along the front of the beach at Lingayen. But it was obvious that the 1st Battalion could never withdraw during a fire fight.

At low tide there was a wide firm strip of sand on the water's edge that changed a few feet inland into deep, clinging sand extending landward several hundred yards. Behind the sand was a spiderweb of canals, channels, dikes, fishtraps, and flooded rice paddies extending several kilometers. There was no route across this maze except one road to Binmaley. The guns had been moved down this road to the firm sand and then manhandled into place. Even our four-by-four trucks could not negotiate that sand. The guns would have to go out the way they came in. If the enemy bombed any one of the countless rickety wooden and bamboo bridges on the Binmaley-beach road, we would literally have our bridges burned behind us. It would also cut off ammunition supply. For that reason I insisted upon moving all available ammunition to the gun area and placing it in small dug-in piles behind the guns.

I wanted the bulk of the ammunition moved several hundred yards farther back to prevent an enemy bomb from touching off the entire supply. Despite my insistence that morning and during repeated daily visits, and despite lip-service agreement by regimental, battalion, and battery commanders, I continued to find the ammunition scattered where it was dumped from the trucks, with a few dead palm branches over the boxes.

The 2nd Battalion, with its wooden-wheeled guns, was in position abreast of Lingayen and of easy access from several directions. But between Lingayen and firm ground was another spiderweb of canals and channels, the principal elements being the Agno River with its myriad of feeders, the Limahong Channel, and a wide swamp crossed only by a narrow causeway.

Between Lingayen and the mouth of the Agno was an island with a shallow-water approach fronted by a maze of fishtraps— a fine obstacle to the night approach of small boats. As the island's close defense was well covered by infantry, I decided to neglect its gun coverage except at far range, and modified the 2nd Battalion's mission accordingly, throwing more weight to the east of Lingayen.

The 3rd Battalion was located well around the perimeter of the bay so that its guns faced east, instead of north, to cover Sual Bay, an important potential landing beach. However, this battalion also had to cover the mouth of the Agno and still be able to fire well to the north toward Bolinao Point—one hell of a mission involving almost a half-circle swing of the guns. Even with this there was a considerable stretch of beach north of Sual Bay, extending to Bolinao, which had absolutely no artillery defense. But hell's bells, we had twenty-four guns stretched thirty miles. I was distressed to learn that this area was undefended by infantry except for periodic patrols.

But, a military force can be stretched just so far, and the seven to eight thousand men of this division were spread butter-thin as it was. It looked from a distance as if a more suitable position to cover Sual Bay could be found to the north. I started in that direction and found to my astonishment that it was almost dusk. I was tired and hungry, and it was too late to make an exhaustive reconnaissance. (Later, a better, if not entirely suitable, position was found to the north.)

Returning to the CP, I caught up with the events of the day.

There was no additional enemy intelligence, but we heard the first rumor of the bombing of Clark Field and Stotsenburg and the incredible statement that our planes had been caught on the ground and destroyed. I refused to believe it.

I hoped to get some rest that night, but soon the entire Lingayen Gulf area was ablaze with rockets, flares, and all sorts of strange lights. It appeared that fifth columnists were well organized and active. Alarm followed alarm, and I fought the telephone system practically all night long, trying to trace down each long-delayed report. Even the area of our own CP was "flared," and we had local guards dashing all over the place. This was to continue nightly, but as we tracked down each light, we met the probable flare shooters who were themselves excitedly looking for traitors.

That night proved conclusively that our communication system was entirely inadequate, and not even satisfactory for simple tactical messages. The glaring fault was the breakdown of switchboard operation. Operators could not understand each other's English, much less that of the American officers. Attempts to use dialect were fruitless. The operators froze mentally and did nothing, least of all answer calls.

I spent the next morning revisiting the battalions while Villa-Real and Bonner tried to get communications workable. They jerked out the switchboards, putting direct lines to each battalion, and started intensive training of the operators, combing the units for men with better education and knowledge of English.

On the night of the 10th I got some rest—my first since war started—from about 10 P.M. until around midnight. There were many flares again, but I was not to be awakened unless something important popped. It popped. The 3rd Battalion reported several dark shapes slowly approaching the mouth of the Agno. I got Savoie on the phone and found him doubtful. He could see nothing definite, but every now and then he thought something was there, almost stationary, or coming in very slowly. It might be tide breaking over a bar. Finally the 2nd Battalion reported "something," and its bearing checked out at about the range Savoie had guessed in the dark. I gave the release to fire and the orders went out. The 3rd Battalion opened up with one battery—the first shot of the war by ground troops of the USAFFE as far as I know.

It was like dropping a match in a warehouse of Fourth of July fireworks. Instantly, Lingayen Gulf was ablaze around its perimeter, as far as the eye could see, with shell bursts, machine-gun tracer bullets, and small arms.

After a few rounds, Savoie reported that he could not see any results, but the shapes could no longer be distinguished. I directed that firing cease, and we were silent the rest of the night. Not so the remainder of the North Luzon Force. Thousands of shadows were killed that night.

In the morning there was no evidence of any sunken ships and a good deal of kidding about shadow shooting. Finally a life preserver with markings which may have been Japanese drifted ashore. Later, USAFFE released a navy dispatch saying a small enemy force passed Bolinao Point and entered Lingayen Gulf that night. Based upon that, the 21st Field Artillery was officially credited with repulsing the first hostile landing attempt. I was skeptical.

However, on the night of December 11 to 12 some small crafts definitely felt their way past Sual Bay, the Agno, Lingayen, Dagupan, and then northward. They drew fire from the 3rd, 2nd, and 1st Battalions in that order. I had no doubt this was a feeler for a possible landing place. The next morning some debris and two light rafts without identifying marks came ashore.

On December 10 General King and Col. Ed Corkill visited us. At dawn of that day I had started out to visit the battalions, and I returned to the CP in the middle of the afternoon filthy, tired, hungry, drawn, and generally low, just as General King arrived.

I took the general to the 1st Battalion since its positions in the heavy sand were our worst and I wanted him to be aware of our situation. He was dissatisfied with the direct fire positions and said I was jeopardizing the guns and crews to enemy aerial and naval bombardment—that before we ever fired a shot, many would be out of action.

I could only justify my decision by citing our lack of training and inadequate communications. I agreed that the exposure of guns and men was everything he said it was but explained as fully as I could my reasoning based on our experience since we had been in position. The general was silent during the remainder of our trip. Afterward, as he reentered his car, he turned to me and said, "I withdraw all my remarks about the beach positions. Your judgment is good. It is a dangerous course but the only one which gives promise of success."

Several days later, as a result of General King's visit, we received our remaining sights, quadrants, and some other fire-control equipment—nowhere the full complement needed, but every bit helped.

The general also gave me some heartbreaking information. We had been hearing rumors about the destruction of Clark Field. King confirmed that the entire complement of planes had been caught on the ground and destroyed. The planes had taken to the air when word of the bombing of Baguio was received, but they came down and were on the apron, their crews at lunch, when the enemy arrived.

The destruction of Clark Field raised a question as to the change, if any, which might be required in our defense plan. MacArthur's plan, which I helped write in 1928 and 1929, was based upon an all-out defense at the beaches. Its promise was that our only chance was to catch the enemy at the period of his greatest weakness—when transports were close in shore, discharging men into small boats. After locating the expedition at sea and determining the beach it was heading for, the navy and air corps would engage the convoy and do as much damage as possible while it was offshore; the shore forces, relying mainly on artillery, would resist the landing, and the infantry would mop up any troops reaching land.

After MacArthur's retirement from active duty, this plan was altered. There would be the same sort of defense at the beach, but in the event of a hostile landing in force, delaying actions were to be fought while the bulk of our forces dropped back to Bataan for a last-ditch stand. The mission of the defense force—unchanged from that of 1928-29—was to hold Corregidor and American sovereignty in the Philippine Islands for six months. MacArthur's original plan was called WPO* No. 1, and the current plan was WPO No. 3. While I was at Stotsenburg in November, we were told that when MacArthur became commander-in-chief the previous summer, he had reverted to the basic plan of WPO No. 1. The principal precampaign difference was the stocking of Bataan with supplies and equipment.

If there could be no air bombardment of transports outside our artillery range, the effectiveness of WPO No. 1 was doubtful. On the other hand, the naval debacle at Pearl Harbor made the arrival of a relief expedition within six months very problematical.

In any event our orders were for an all-out, last-ditch defense at the beach. There was no doubt of this in my mind until we received a visit from Colonel Irwin, USAFFE G-3 (operations). When I took him to the 2nd and 1st Battalions, he looked at our ammunition disposition and the dangerous supply routes and violently announced it would be impossible to withdraw the ammunition in time to save it, and by God he would crucify anyone who lost as much as one round.

This was the first time we heard the word "withdraw." I explained to him that our orders were to hold at all costs; that we had only 200 rounds per gun at the positions, less than one

*War Plan Orange.—Ed.

full day of fire. I emphasized the orders received for the last-ditch defense, repeating one grandiloquent expression of the North Luzon Force order: "We must die in our tracks, falling, not backward but forward, toward the enemy."

Irwin's answer was, "Don't believe everything you hear. As God is my judge, if you leave one round of ammunition behind for the enemy, I'll have your head."

After Irwin left we had a conference to review our mission. We were committed to final defense at the beach. It was physically impossible to withdraw from the beach during action. Now we had, at least by implication, an entirely different or amplified mission. We tried to get a decision from North Luzon Force but received only a reiteration of the hold-at-all-cost order.

As a result we were straddling the fence. In an attempt to fight at the beach and yet be prepared for withdrawal, we sent one battery from the beach to a rearward position, along with the bulk of the battalion ammunition, placing it in dumps along the main axis of withdrawal. By thus preparing to withdraw, we sacrificed combat efficiency and jeopardized our assigned mission. But in the state of flux, I could see no other solution.

On December 14 Catalan and I came under fire for the first time. We were in the command car, its motor laboring noisily in the heavy sand near Binmaley, when we heard the squeal of a diving plane and the staccato drum of machine guns. Sand kicked up around us. Before we realized we were being strafed, it was all over; the plane was out over the bay. We took the top of the command car down and never put it up again.

During the next few days we heard rumors of fighting near Vigan, where the enemy had landed earlier, and San Fernando La Union, but no definite news. Flares continued nightly, with much evidence of fifth column activities. Toward the end of the campaign, I learned that telegrams had been dispatched from the Lingayen Bureau of Posts to USAFFE over my name and Catalan's stating that the 21st Field Artillery was disorganized, demoralized, and would not stand to the guns in case of attack. They concluded with a recommendation that the regiment be disbanded, the men be returned to their homes, and no resistance be attempted. I have no idea what reception the telegrams had at headquarters. Later events caused me to believe they were sent by an officer of the regiment. The order to withdraw was received the morning of December 24, and we pulled out at dark. I visited all battalions and checked the arrangements, and had nothing to do afterward except worry that the enemy would interfere, so I brought my diary up to date. Here is what had happened:

Late on the 20th-21st we received a message from USAFFE through division that a Japanese expedition of one hundred to one hundred and twenty vessels, escorted by warships, was moving south toward Lingayen Gulf and could be expected off the mouth of the gulf by dark on the 21st. This was the moment we had been awaiting. I assembled the battalion commanders, their key staff members, and the regimental staff. I explained to them the fundamentals of the defense plan—the joint army, navy, and air corps action. I stressed that a large part of the task would devolve on us because of the loss of planes during the Clark Field attack, and cautioned that the attempt to land would be preceded by a tremendous bombardment from air and water. I was pleased with everyone's attitude—calm, determined, rather grave, but relieved that the test was finally to come.

In the late afternoon of the 21st, we received information that a few vessels had been maneuvering near Vigan during the day, but that the main expedition was turning in from sea toward the gulf and landing operations could be expected at dawn. With confidence in the leadership and brilliant strategy of MacArthur, who had been on my pedestal since 1928, I awaited the dawn. I was awakened long before daylight, checked all communications, talked to all CPs, and again cautioned extreme alertness.

Came the dawn—and the enemy vessels—but not a shot, not a bomb, not a torpedo from our side. From the 2nd Battalion CP atop the capitol building at Lingayen, the huge fleet of hostile vessels could be seen far to the north and near the eastern shore in the vicinity of San Fernando. But neither at dawn nor during the morning did we see an American bomber or observe any action by the enemy fleet that would indicate the presence of American submarines. If there was any defense against the landing, it was purely local and so far away that we could not hear it.

During the day we received the news that the enemy main force landed practically unopposed from Vigan to San Fernando. Heartsick and despondent, I felt the impending hand of disaster. Apparently there had been no effort to effect the basic defense plan; no opportunity to attack the enemy convoy. I realized that if we did not have sufficient air strength to assist us in this critical period, the remainder of our campaign would be under the eyes of Japanese aviators. We would be constantly pinned to the earth, all daylight movement paralyzed. Observers in Europe had told of the disintegration of the Polish, French, Belgian, Dutch, and British armies under the unopposed attacks of the German air force. Could this newly levied, partially equipped, and inexperienced army perform the miracle those experienced armies found impossible?

The picture was pretty dark—but hope dies hard. The situation wasn't so unfavorable. The hostile landing was in a narrow corridor, with water on one side and precipitous mountains on the other. The corridor was crossed by many streams that formed good delaying lines. To the south the terrain became favorable for a concerted counterattack. At the proper moment a vigorous attack could wipe the invaders out of the corridor, and the navy and aircraft bombing could ensure that their line of retreat via the sea would be cut off. We had available the 11th, 21st, 71st, and 91st Divisions. In addition, I presumed our best troops, the Philippine Division* in army reserve, were close enough to be brought up quickly to spearhead the attack. I felt there was a distinct possibility that the 21st Division

*A long-service, professional unit composed of U.S. Army regulars and Philippine Scout troops.—Ed.

would sideslip to take place in the attack, and most certainly the 21st's artillery would be pulled to the east to take part. I made a hasty road reconnaissance toward Damortis, alerted the battalions, and awaited orders. None came. Instead, an alarming number of stragglers began coming through our area, and with them the story of what happened on the right flank.

Our force only had patrols in the Vigan area, from an infantry battalion stationed near San Fernando and commanded by a Major Noble. The Vigan landings of December 10 to 14 were unopposed except by local Constabulary and home guard detachments. On the 16th the enemy began pushing southward. There were several small actions until the main forces came into contact near San Fernando La Union shortly before the major landing took place. The Japanese must also have pushed up the Tagudin trail toward Cervantes and Baguio, for stragglers told of action there. As the main enemy force landed and moved to the south, a combat team was sent to help Noble—a battalion with some self-propelled artillery.

This force was sent forward in big red buses. There were no reconnaissance jeeps, command or patrol cars, or radio cars. The junior officers must have been inexperienced in patrolling, for the stragglers' story was that they went forward en masse, neglecting the vital principle of security. The leading elements hit the enemy and went into action, very quickly discovering they had passed, without reconnoitering, a side road that paralleled the coast highway. At the time, the head of the column ran into a hostile ambuscade, heavy with mortars, machine guns, and light portable artillery. The side road was filled with enemy troops. They disgorged from that road and the combat team was cut off.

Another expedition, this time a regiment or a regiment less a battalion, motored forward. This force went cautiously and apparently met with some initial success until Japanese naval vessels moved in, shelling the hell out of them, while additional forces were landing from transports still farther south, making a four-layer, three-decker sandwich out of our troops. The appearance of Japanese tanks completed the picture. Some individuals escaped to the mountains and then back to the main body in the plains. One of the Del Pilar officers, with tears in his eyes, told us of pushing the SPMs off a cliff on the Naguilian trail. Somewhere in this scheme of things the 26th Cavalry must have been in the action, for we had riderless horses and cavalry stragglers coming through. One 26th Cavalry sergeant told me of being chased down the road by a small tank, not much bigger than a motorcycle and sidecar.

All these tales were of piecemeal commitments of relatively small units. We heard nothing of the 11th, 71st, or 91st Divisions engaging as divisions or as part of a larger force. I hoped they were still cohesive. But if the main force of our troops was still unengaged, I could account for the withdrawal order. An American infantry officer told me the enemy had debouched into the Pangasanan plains and the right flank of the army was imperiled. If this was so, the enemy had moved with incredible speed in forty-eight hours: landing troops, artillery, tanks, and transport and supplies; driving off opposition, forcing a difficult defile, and debouching into the open. This was military efficiency of top grade.

I feared the presence of the stragglers presaged disaster. We formed them up and sent them to division, but I felt sure few arrived there. Their stories were the same: always the storyteller was subjected to terrible mortar fire; always he continued bravely to fire his rifle, machine gun, or 75; always his officers ran away—or if the teller was an officer, his superior officers ran first; always the enemy planes dropped many bombs and fired many machine guns; always there suddenly appeared many hostile tanks headed straight for him; always he was suddenly astonished to realize he was absolutely alone, all others having run away or been killed. Then and only then, with the tanks a few feet away, had he flung himself to one side where . . . Here the story had two variations. First, he was captured but escaped that night; second, he hid until night, when he returned to our lines. But the story didn't stop; from there the threads reunited. The stragglers were very tired, they sought their companions, they were very hungry, and, sir, could they be transferred to the Motor Transport Corps and drive a truck?

Several times on December 24 enemy vessels moved in toward Lingayen and Binmaley. Harrison gave me periodic reports from his CP on the capitol dome. The ships were about 3,000 yards beyond our gun range, maneuvering slowly. I expected they would put a force ashore at dusk. If they did, it would be just as we were pulling the guns back across the maze of canals and bottlenecks, and there would be hell to pay. The only thing I could see to do was sit tight and fight the guns. I had a copy of the force withdrawal order and oral orders of the division plan. The force plan was to withdraw, starting at 7 P.M. on the 24th; to occupy a delaying position before dawn, holding it during daylight; and to withdraw again the next night, continuing the procedure until the final defensive line was reached. Our division was to withdraw on two roads, one east of the Agno, until the big bend of the river near Camiling was reached; thereafter we were to form in one column. The lack of bridges and communication across the Agno made it impossible for the two columns to give mutual support.

The force order required that the rear of each column be covered by a shell* to remain in position each night until just before dawn, when it was to withdraw rapidly to rejoin the division. One battalion of field artillery was to remain with each shell—one-third of the division artillery strength. This was out of proportion to the infantry in the shells—about the equivalent of one company—and the infantry strength was not sufficient to protect the guns if the enemy advanced vigorously.

*By "shell" the author means a covering (or rear guard) force.—Ed.

The first two of our withdrawal phase lines coincided with the positions I had selected and pointed out in the terrain study I presented to the officers during our training period. The delaying positions for the 21st Division were:

D-1—from the Zambales range down a spur to the vicinity of Aguilar, then across the Agno River;

D-2—from the Zambales down another spur near Mangaterem and across the Agno;

D-3—the flat open ridge line near our old camp at Sta. Ignacia and across the Agno;

D-4—south of the Tarlac River, south of Tarlac along the south bank of a small stream extending eastward along the Tarlac-La Pas Road;

D-5—(the final line to be held at all costs)—from the Zambales north of Stotsenburg along the high ground north of the Bamban River, then across the river at a point near the highway, then south of the Bamban, and finally refusing the right flank back toward Mt. Arayat and the Candaba swamp.

Back in my Stotsenburg days I had gone over the final line many times. D-5 was a fine strong line in most respects, but like any defensive position had disadvantages. It had a good field of fire, excellent artillery observation, was well anchored to mountains on both flanks, and had a large portion of the center covered by an impenetrable swamp which, however, was not deep enough to be a barrier to our own lateral line of communication. It had the disadvantage of being long, requiring a very large number of troops to defend it, although it was the shortest line between Lingayen and Manila. It was very open terrain, leaving us very much exposed to air attack. But its principal weakness was that its rear, toward Manila, had to be defended against attacks from the southern Luzon beaches, or in certain circumstances, from Manila Bay.

From all I could gather from division, Manila was still the key point we were to defend to the end on D-5. Presumably, the South Luzon Force had a similar line south of Manila. Although I heard of some supplies being moved to Bataan, the

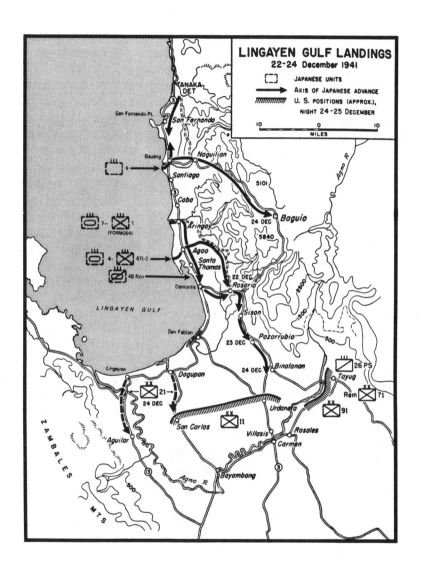

LINGAYEN GULF LANDINGS
22-24 December 1941

JAPANESE UNITS

AXIS OF JAPANESE ADVANCE

U. S. POSITIONS (APPROX.),
NIGHT 24-25 DECEMBER

10   0   10
MILES

bulk still was in Manila. Of course, Bataan also was covered by the D-5 line.

At 7 P.M. on December 24 the command post closed and was set in motion to the rear. Catalan and I waited for the regiment to pass on the road. After eons of anxiety we heard the rumble of the 2nd Battalion's wooden wheels. We counted the six trailed guns as they went past us, and then our homemade self-propelled mount platoon. These were naval three-inch guns bolted to the back of some flatbed trucks in accordance with suggestions I had made to Harrison. Harrison brought up the rear and told us the withdrawal was without incident, only the wire crews being behind him. One third of the regiment was safely out of the labyrinth. Much later—far longer than I anticipated would be necessary—one battery of the 3rd Battalion passed us. At the rear the battalion commander, Lieutenant Acosta, checked in. His withdrawal was also uneventful, and one battery had gone into position with the infantry shell. The American instructor, Lieutenant Savoie, had elected to stay with that battery. Everything was out to our knowledge except the 1st Battalion and the wire trucks. The 1st Battalion would be out of touch for several days; so, with a prayer for them, Catalan and I started to follow the rear of the regiment to the CP Villa-Real and Bonner had selected south of Mangaterem.

Unfortunately, the division staff officer had not assigned locations for the division service units, and when we arrived we found the 21st Engineers had picked our CP location for their bivouac area. They had a madhouse of red trucks parked in the open, with picks, shovels, trunk lockers, and kitchen equipment piled indiscriminately, just as they had been thrown from the trucks. Most of the men and all the officers were asleep in nearby *nipa* shacks. With some difficulty I found an officer, awoke him, and persuaded him to get his impedimenta under cover. Daylight found everything under cover, at least after a fashion.

It was Christmas Eve. I spread my bedroll alongside my car and got about three hours' sleep. I turned out at daylight and

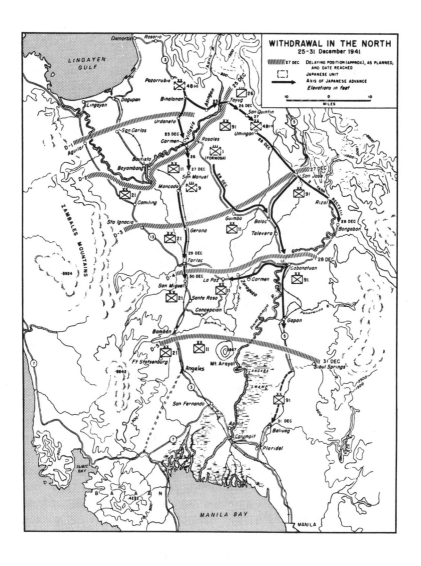

WITHDRAWAL IN THE NORTH
25-31 December 1941

spent a moment thinking of past Christmas mornings. After a rather sketchy breakfast and a check-in at division CP—where we found no new information about the situation on either the right or the front—Catalan and I went to look at the battalion areas. I was not very happy about the energy displayed in contacting the infantry front lines and preparing to support them. Lack of experience and a weak sense of responsibility had resulted in their positioning the guns, and that was all. How the guns were to be laid* and fired, how the fire missions would be known, and how the fires would be conducted— these things had not been considered by the battalion commanders. We initiated them, visited infantry units, and then returned to our CP.

Bernado was spit-roasting an eight-pound turkey, but at that time we were told that the division commander wanted us. Reluctantly leaving the rest of the officers at their Christmas mess, we headed for division CP.

There we found that the news from the right flank was bad, but the situation was so obscure that it was impossible to evaluate how bad. General Capinpin† told us the withdrawal to line D-2 at 7 P.M. would be according to schedule and gave us a force order to read. The order attached two self-propelled mount batteries to the 21st Division and suggested that they be used as the artillery ordered to support the covering forces. Accordingly, Capinpin constituted an artillery groupment consisting of two SPM batteries and the 21st Field Artillery and placed me in command of it.

This was a godsend, for it gave me the authority to issue commands instead of recommendations and suggestions. Before that time I had been issuing commands—no doubt of that —but I had been trying my damndest to do so only in the

*A term meaning orientation of the battery's several guns so that they shoot in a parallel sheaf and in the desired direction.—Ed.

†The promotion of this officer to brigadier general, mentioned earlier, had by now occurred.—Ed.

absence of Catalan or in cases of emergency. When he was present I waited for him to act, when that was possible, but then issued the orders when it became apparent that action was not forthcoming. Even so, I tried always to cloak the orders as suggestions and asked Catalan for his agreement. When dealing with battalion commanders, I attempted to convey the idea that I was issuing orders as a staff officer *for* him by prefacing the order with "Colonel Catalan directs . . ." or "The regimental commander wishes . . ." Nevertheless, and despite constant effort to be tactful, I am afraid that at times I was pretty roughshod.

The two SPM batteries were at Camiling and at the new engineer bridge at the ford of the Agno north of Camiling (Wawa). I sent messages to Lieutenant Fisher, commanding the Wawa battery, directing him to contact the 21st Division column, which was withdrawing east of the Agno, and to cover its retirement across the Wawa bridge; I directed Lieutenant Svodbodny, the American officer commanding the battery at Camiling, to come to my CP. I intended to send him north on Route 13 to cover the rear of the division's main body. But before we left division CP, and after the messenger had gone, we received rumors of hostile tanks in the rear of the 11th Division and on the flank of the next withdrawal of the 21st. So when Svodbodny reported, I ordered him to remain at Camiling, contacting Fisher and covering the right and rear of the division against tanks. We returned to the CP and had our Christmas dinner, sitting on the running board of the car. There was an eight-pound turkey for about twenty of us, supplemented with canned pork and beans and topped off with slivers from a two-ounce can of cheddar cheese. A bottle of Scotch divided among twelve of us provided the festive touch.

After dinner I went through Camiling to see Fisher, stopping at division for any late news. An officer who had returned from the 11th Division said the situation looked critical. Stragglers from the 71st Infantry confirmed the disintegration of that regiment and also that the 26th Cavalry had been pretty roughly handled near Damortis. A regiment of the 91st Division had been cut to pieces near Pozorrubio, and a battalion of artillery had been captured. The troops in the Cagayan Valley were in danger of being cut off if their only route of withdrawal via Balete Pass was cut. Tanks were reported in and around the right flank and rear. Of more immediate concern, the covering shell left the previous night at the Bugallon triangle was not yet heard from.

I abandoned the idea of visiting Fisher's battery and started forward to find out what I could about the shell and, with it, my battery. As I reached the artillery area the battery passed me, and I contacted Savoie after chasing him for a few kilometers. He had reached the D-1 line a few minutes before 7 P.M., in time to join the main column, leaving the other battery of the battalion in position. Acosta was with the battalion, protected by the new shell.

Catalan and I again checked the column past us and then followed it to the new area behind the D-2 line, arriving about 10 P.M. Our CP was in the graveyard at Camiling.

That night, for the first time during the campaign, I had a bad case of jitters. I had finished the last war in the hospital* convalescing for my return to the front and had not been able to practice the doctrine preached among horsemen—after a bad fall, mount up immediately and ride again. I probably left the hospital with a mild case of shell shock. Be that as it may, for twenty years I had been living with the vague fear that should another war occur, I might break under heavy shell fire and end my military career in disgrace. Until that night at Camiling, I had been too busy to think about it. But there, among the gravestones and several open tombs, I could not sleep. I knew from the last war that no man alive can go through heavy shell fire without fear, but only the weak give way to that fear. I realized my personal test could not be far off, and I was

*Suffering from severe mustard gas burns.—Ed.

afraid—almost to the panic stage—that I would not measure up. I was bathed in a cold sweat. Just then occurred two of the loudest explosions I have ever heard. With the paucity of information about our right flank and rear, these explosions could have meant almost anything. I shook from head to foot and was incapable of making a decision had one been required of me. I finally reasoned that the explosions were the blowing up of the railroad and highway bridges at Bayambang. Comforted, I dropped off to sleep. Strangely, this incident greatly strengthened and encouraged me. I had a new feeling of confidence.

Early in the morning of December 26, Catalan and I checked the front line, finding things much the same as the day before —positions good, but prospects of giving fire support to the infantry very poor because of lack of communication, faulty liaison, and insufficient energy. Leaving Catalan to improve the situation, I went through Camiling to see Fisher's SPM battery at Wawa and Svodbodny's at Camiling. I found that the east column of the 21st Division, including the shell and shell battery, was already south of the big bend of the Agno. While I was delighted to see that Hendry and Valdez had come through the maze of bottlenecks safely, I was disturbed by the location of the line. The main body of the division west of the Agno was several miles advanced to the north with its flank in the air, expecting the line east of the Agno to prolong its own.

Fisher's position was good, his guns covering the temporary bridge that had been partially destroyed. I returned to Camiling and ordered Svodbodny to move one platoon east on the Camiling-Gerona road, to find the division right flank in its new location, and to cover it from tank attack.

When I returned to the CP I heard a wild rumor. After the customary rearward reconnaissance, Bonner had continued back to North Luzon Force CP at Bamban in an attempt to get telephone wire and other signal equipment. There he heard a staff officer say USAFFE had decided not to attempt the last-ditch defense on D-5, but to retire into Bataan. Then the Filipinos, except Scouts, were to be demobilized, declared

civilians, and returned to their homes. The Americans and the
Philippine Division would defend Bataan as long as possible,
then retire to Corregidor and await the relief expedition.

There was a possibility of truth to this rumor. The inex-
perience, lack of training, and equipment deficiencies of the
Philippine army made it plausible that the high command had
decided—the army having put up an honorable and courageous
resistance to the limit of its ability—further bloodshed would
be useless.

Although I doubted it, and could not see the Filipinos con-
senting to such a plan, I had to place enough credence in it to
be prepared. There at Camiling I burned all my private papers,
letters from my family, other correspondence, and all except
official material pertaining to the campaign.

Since there was only one road south from Camiling, the
division planned to move the 23rd, 21st, and 22nd Infantries
in that order, with the covering force of the 21st to the west of
the road and that of the 22nd to the east. My plan to conform
was simple: I had only one road to cover and a regiment and
two SPM batteries to do it with. I ordered the 21st Artillery to
move out intact in order of battalions 2, 3, and 1. Svodbodny
was to hold his position at Camiling, then join the division's
covering shell as soon as Fisher's battery passed through him.
Fisher was to push south to the vicinity of Sta. Ignacia and
cover the trail from the east across the Tarlac River.

I visited Fisher again in the late afternoon and authorized
him to fire at the temporary bridge just before he withdrew.
The bridge had been blown by the engineers but the destruction was incomplete. A large number of stragglers, many of
them wounded, had been collected at Fisher's battery. I loaded
the wounded into a truck and started the stragglers for the rear.

Just before retirement, Fisher opened up to destroy the
bridge. He had barely finished when several big red buses drove
up to the far side of the bridge, and their occupants swam and
waded over to our side of the bridge. They were the remnants
of a battalion of the 21st Infantry that had been in action near

Villasis, Rosales, and the Carmen bridge. The battalion had serious losses in severe fighting and was badly disorganized.

When I returned to Camiling and the CP, I found everything changed. Instead of going back cross-country and then via Route 13, the 22nd would retire by both Route 13 and the Mantla North road. I was ordered by division to cover the rear of the latter column.

During the day I picked up an extra SPM gun, an ammunition truck, and a command pickup, which three American soldiers had brought to Camiling from the ordnance shops at Manila. Their battery, which had been with the South Luzon Force, had been ordered to Camiling but never arrived. I first attached the gun to Svodbodny, but he did not have enough gunners to handle it, so I got a crew from the 2nd Battalion of the 21st and formed a provisional SPM battery with this gun and our two homemade SPMs, placing Harrison in command. I sent orders to Catalan to have this provisional battery take over Fisher's mission on the Sta. Ignacia–Tarlac River trail.

As the withdrawal began, I watched the column past the Camiling crossroads, catching Fisher and giving him new orders —which were to conclude by his going into bivouac near St. Quintin when the shell pulled back to D-3 at dawn. His battery needed rest and food.

Following the column south, I was stopped in Sta. Ignacia by Lt. Maury Day III, who had orders to report to me with another SPM battery. I was delighted, for that gave me the means of covering the south, or rear, of the division. I sent Day south across the Tarlac River bridge to cover the bridge bottleneck against attack from the south and southeast.

Our new CP was in the vicinity of that bridge. Sometime after midnight explosions were heard toward Tarlac. Fearing Svodbodny was in a jam, I went into Tarlac. The railroad yards there had been bombed, although we had heard no planes. Tarlac was being looted. Catalan and I tried to stop it until several shop owners told us they had thrown what was left of their stocks open to the soldiers rather than let the enemy have anything. Catalan and I bought—yes, bought—some cigars and a half-dozen bottles of beer, which we shared with Bonner and Villa-Real.

Catalan and I visited the battalions the next morning (December 27) and found everything in fine shape, but during the afternoon we had a near panic. Planes had been over us all morning, continuing to bomb Tarlac. Suddenly there were a number of explosions, sounding like 75s, to our rear toward Tarlac. My surmise was that the planes had guided tanks toward us and Lieutenant Day had gone into action. Within a few minutes, Luna, the division G-3, came breathlessly to tell us he had seen Japanese soldiers in the dry bed of the Tarlac River. I asked him to send some infantry from the nearby reserve regiment to Day's flanks. We were in a cul-de-sac, the steep banks of the river behind us, a trail into the hill jungle to our right, the bridge bottleneck to our left, and the enemy in front—if you could consider the division rear a front. To add to the confusion, three hostile bombers began circling overhead. We formed our headquarters personnel, using their rifles for local defense and taking cover behind a hedge fence.

Nothing happened. The explosions stopped. Finally, I started walking up the road toward Day's position. Two American infantry officers had the same idea and caught up with me in a car. I hopped on the running board. We found Day alert, but he hadn't fired. The explosions had been the Pantranco Bus Company blowing up its gasoline tanks to prevent the fuel from falling into enemy hands. The enemy soldiers in the river had been a figment of Luna's imagination.

With a prayer that I might never again be caught in such a design for disaster, I went back to the CP to get ready to move at 7 P.M. There I found Svodbodny. During the morning I had visited him near Gerona and ordered him back to the northern exit of Tarlac to cover both the Manila North road and the Tarlac–La Paz road on which hostile tanks were reported. He did, but received a peremptory written message: "Return your guns to Gerona without delay. Remain there until the last tank has retired through your position. By Command of Brigadier General Weaver. R. C. Pettit, Jr., Captain, ADC."

I had never heard of General Weaver. On investigation, I found him to be in command of a group of two battalions of light tanks. I did not know what authority he had, if any, over my guns, but that was of no importance—the main thing was that there was an apparent need for the guns. I ordered Svodbodny to comply with the message until I could reconcile the conflict of authority. I had no objection to protecting tanks, but if there had to be a choice between protecting tanks and protecting infantry, there was no doubt as to my assigned mission.

I went looking for General Weaver and found him with a command tank and half-track on the North road between Tarlac and Gerona. I introduced myself and explained my mission and my orders for employing the SPMs. The general was under pretty high tension, as well he might be from the kicking around his tanks were getting, and was quite hostile to me. He said he was operating directly under USAFFE; that North Luzon Force orders did not affect him; that the SPMs were directly and absolutely under his command; and that their sole reason for existence was to protect his tanks.

I restated my position—that the SPMs were placed under my command by my superiors—and asked him to reconcile the conflict of command. I emphasized, however, that there was only one war and that I would give his tanks every support consistent with my mission. I agreed to leave Svodbodny temporarily with him at Gerona. Eventually, we worked out a joint employment of the SPMs which contented the tank people even if it didn't make them entirely happy.

At 7 P.M. we withdrew to D-4 without incident. Catalan and I checked the battalion positions selected by Bonner and Villa-Real. The 3rd Battalion was west of the highway by a barrio near the Tarlac Airfield. It was too close to the road and could not reach far enough to the west, into the rolling hill country, where hostile attack was probable. The terrain there was very favorable for an enemy attack which could drive a wedge between the Zambales River and our main force. This would deprive us of the mountain anchor for our left flank, jeopardizing our retirement to the D-5 position or our chance of getting around the point of the mountains from where we would have to turn southwest to get into Bataan.

The next morning, December 28, I checked the SPM positions and at Harrison's battery had my first meal in several days—a breakfast consisting of a can of tomato juice, a can of corned beef, and a canteen cup half full of Scotch. Then I revisited the 3rd battalion and Fisher's battery and became more uneasy about the open left flank and our failure to have it within range of our guns. I visited division CP with my tank troubles and fears about the left flank. Colonel O'Day agreed with me, but General Capinpin and the rest of the staff felt that everything was fine, just fine.

When I returned to the CP I found Bonner back from North Luzon Force CP—this time with orders, not rumors. He carried a copy of a hastily written message from Montgomery:

"Commanding General, all divisions.

"D-5 is abandoned as a final defensive line. D-4 will be held at all costs until ordered withdrawn. Maximum delay will be effected on each position. Withdrawal plan later. Wainwright."

Montgomery had told Bonner that D-4 would have to be held for several days.

As I finished reading this message, Savoie telephoned to say that Japanese bicyclists had been observed in Tarlac, enemy patrols were reported near Route 13 south of the Tarlac River bridge, and many Japanese were working southward along the foothills of the Zambales north of the Tarlac. As yet there was no contact.

The message and the telephone call added up to the fact that we would have to hold out longer than we had anticipated on D-4 and that our flank was being felt out—in short, we would have to fight, not delay, on our present line.

Cursing the complacency that had left our vital flank up in the air, I went with Catalan to division CP. The news had been received there, as well as the information that Wappenstein, commanding the 21st Infantry, was extending his line toward the mountain on his own initiative.

Catalan concurring, orders were issued to our 3rd Battalion to move its gun positions to the west to cover the left flank and support Wappenstein. Both Acosta, the battalion commander, and Savoie, the instructor, demurred, saying the terrain was unfavorable. As a matter of fact, the terrain was the most favorable for artillery we had yet had, with rolling hills and good cover. The difficulty was the lack of roads. Savoie was as good an American officer as I had, and I considered Acosta the best battalion commander. Yet, I was disappointed in them and brusque in my insistence that they get their guns where they could be effective, come hell or high water.

The 3rd Battalion moved during the night of December 28 to 29. The morning arrived without contact. Catalan and I took a more detailed look at all units except the 3rd Battalion.

December 29 will always be memorable to me for three things: the ROTC boys, the beginning of aerial operations against our troops, and the first serious contact with the enemy. I stopped my car near Capas to talk to Harrison. About thirty youngsters swarmed over my car—boys in ROTC uniform and students from various schools in and near Manila. They wanted me to tell them what to do. When war started, they had gone into intensive training toward a commission, proudly and with much waving of banners. On the 26th their schools were closed, their units were disbanded, and they were told to go home. Their homes were in Lingayen, Dagupan, Sta. Barbara, La Union, the Bontoc—all in Japanese hands; their families were probably scattered. In any event, they could not get through the lines in uniform without danger. I advised them to return to Manila. "But, sir, everyone is leaving Manila. They tell us the Japanese will be there today or tomorrow."

I had nothing more to offer them. For two days I passed and repassed this group at the same point, the number dwindling each time. I had Harrison feed them once or twice. They sat dejectedly along the road, homeless and abandoned. When we passed for the last time on our withdrawal, they were gone. I wondered where. The memory of one boy, about the age of my son Bill, with the same big brown eyes, quick grin, and big lock of wavy, unruly hair, haunted me for days.

Strangely enough, enemy aircraft had not yet been active against our troops, despite a thousand remunerative targets. On the 29th they started working on our columns, groups of vehicles, and assembly areas. A group of nine dive bombers became active that day and continued to be. They were led by one plane with a knocking whine in its motor, easily identified. Daily, almost hourly, I played hide and seek, blindman's bluff, and drop the handkerchief with it. I developed a fine technique for diving into ditches, culverts, under bridges, and into V trenches. It reduced my mobility very materially. We named it Herman; why, I cannot say, except for ease of reference and cursing.

(Herman remained our constant companion into and on Bataan. He and his group blasted us out of three CPs, killed a number of our men and wounded more, and was effective mainly in limiting our daylight movement. Without aerial or antiaircraft opposition, he could come low enough, figuratively, to lift the tree branches and look underneath before spitting his bombs. A most effective member of the Imperial Japanese Air Force.)

Reports came hourly from Wappenstein, Savoie, and Acosta telling of increasing pressure as the enemy felt out our left flank. Wappenstein was badly overextended and still was not as far to the west as he wanted to go. His regiment had only two battalions, and one had taken such rough handling as to be incapable of further action. Savoie was frantic. He and Acosta were as far west as they could push their guns with the old single-axle drive trucks, and there were still miles of open country, undulating and defiladed, beyond gun range, giving the enemy an unobstructed route around our left flank and to the bottleneck from Angeles to Porac. The infantry line in front of Savoie was so thin he had trouble finding it.

I was heartsick over the possibility of losing the battalion. I knew Acosta and Savoie felt I was wrong in forcing them into positions so far from the highway. I began to doubt my own judgment. With the force falling to pieces on the right, and the necessity of getting as many guns into Bataan as possible, was I justified in trying to make a fight out of it on this line to comply with the corps' directive of maximum delay?

I went again to division, and from Montgomery, North Luzon Force, assistant G-3, I learned that the enemy was in contact along the entire line from Tarlac to Cabanatuan. The 71st Division, badly disorganized, had been pulled off the line and was reorganizing at reduced strength. The 11th Division had lost one regiment and part of another in the fighting around and north of Damortis. It had no organic artillery, and the artillery of the other two divisions had lost a good many guns, as had the SPMs.

It was imperative that the North Luzon Force keep the Manila-San Fernando-Guagua highway until the South Luzon Force could withdraw. This was estimated to be midnight of January 1 to 2 at the earliest—three-and-a-half days. It was emphasized that the D-4 line must be held at all costs until the order to withdraw was issued. After that withdrawal, the 21st Division was to go into bivouac near Pilar, on the east coast of Bataan.

In response to my questions, Montgomery added—no telephone wire was available; no radio sets were available; no machine guns, antiaircraft, or otherwise were available; no field artillery fire-control equipment was available; no topographical equipment was available. The D-5 line had not been staked out; the exact line had to be selected by the division. No airplane photos or mosaics were available. There were plenty of maps at the G-3 office in the stone church at Bacolor, some of them Spanish dating from 1892, most of them 1907 editions. None scaled 1/20,000, and not one was worth a tinker's damn.

I asked about reserves to be moved up behind our left flank in case the enemy broke out between Wappenstein and the Zambales. Montgomery answered that North Luzon Force had no reserves except what was left of the 26th Cavalry, and that the situation on the right was so precarious there was question of moving them to the left.

After Montgomery left we tried to evaluate the situation. The hostile pressure was severe. Our tanks were being employed tactically as machine-gun nests, covering critical road junctions and terrain. I felt they might better be used en masse for counterattacks to relieve critical pressure, but I was not a tank man. They were taking heavy losses. Through their radio we received information that hostile tanks were massing north of Tarlac and La Paz. Thus, we had not only the division left flank to worry about, but the right flank—a fine tank avenue— between Tarlac and La Paz as well.

We discussed first the left flank. The force insistence on the defense of D-4 made me feel better about my decision to push Acosta and Savoie toward the west and make a fight out of it on the D-4 line.

There was a distinct gap between the right flank of the 21st Division and the left of the 11th Division. This was discussed. From time immemorial a general's nightmare has been a turned flank. Now we had the prospect of a turned left flank and a penetration between divisions, which, in effect, would mean a turned right flank. Yet the estimate of the situation was that we were doing all possible and that we would sit tight and await developments.

I returned to the regimental CP in my car. Herman was very active. Several times I became aware of his presence by seeing people dive for ditches. On one occasion I did not have the benefit of the bystanders, and, as a result, I set the world's record for the sitting-sideways broad jump. In a few days it became automatic to cut the switches, jerk the handbrake (in hope that the car would stop before climbing a tree), flip open the door, and dive for the nearest cover—all in one motion.

In the late afternoon Herman and his companions bombed the reserve regiment adjacent to our CP at Sta. Rosa. A nice little job neatly done. None of the bombs came nearer to us than a hundred yards, but it was very unpleasant. I was not happy.

Fisher, of the SPMs, had an infected toe. Blood poisoning set in and he was forced to go to the hospital, turning his battery over to George Reed, whom I had at Sta. Ignacia during the training period before the war. I was to miss Fisher. He had something so sadly lacking in many officers—the will to fight.

The night of December 29 to 30 was reasonably quiet, despite my fear of action against the left. On the 30th orders came for Svodbodny, who was with me at the time, to move without delay to Calumpit for antitank protection. Speed, although not specifically ordered, was certainly indicated. An hour later a frantic call came. "Where is Svodbodny?" I went to his positions and found him just pulling out. My only criticism of Svodbodny was that he was overdeliberate: not slow, not overcautious, but on the phlegmatic side. Nevertheless, he was an excellent officer of absolute fearlessness.

During the day, Wappenstein, Warren, Savoie, and Acosta were in almost constant communication with us. The story was the same—the enemy building up and feeling his way to the west, seeking our left flank. Also, pressure was being built up frontally along the continuation of Route 13 to the southeast. There was sporadic mortar and machine-gun fire from Tarlac for several kilometers to the west.

Several organized attacks developed, but Savoie repeatedly called me to report jubilantly, "Colonel, they break out and come toward us. We open up and slap a few rounds at them and they fold right back one hell of a sight faster than they come out." This is an expurgated account of his remarks. Savoie was a red-headed, volatile, nervous Louisianan of, I imagined, French-Creole extraction. He became so excited it was sometimes difficult to understand his rapid, high-pitched voice. He did not really curse; expletives simply constituted a major portion of his normal conversation.

Wappenstein was high in his praise of Savoie, telling me once that the boy was holding the line almost by himself, that the infantry line was so thin there wasn't the ghost of a chance of it holding had not the artillery fire kept breaking up the attacks. This report reestablished my confidence in my judgment. If the guns had not been moved westward, they could not have reached the area of the attacks.

About 3 P.M. Savoie reported a strong attack developing on the left. Hendry reported a similar attack developing in the woods northeast of Tarlac, and Reed told me of many Japanese in the southern part of Tarlac and around the capital buildings.

At about the same time, we received orders to withdraw to D-5 at 7 P.M. With difficulty, because of poor communication, I got the withdrawal order to all units, reaching the 3rd Battalion in the middle of the toughest fire fight of the day. While I talked with them about the progress of the fight, the line went out.

Just then the Japanese started pouring out of Tarlac toward the 22nd Infantry. Because of uncertainty as to the exact location of the 11th Division's left flank, orders had been given that authority to fire had to come from either Catalan or myself. Hendry now asked for authority to fire, but he could not positively identify the advancing troops. He could not see them, but his observers were certain they were hostile. Colonel O'Day cut in on the wire—we were using the commercial trunk line—with orders not to fire, that the troops were the 13th Infantry.

A few seconds later Hendry called again: the 22nd was firing and McCafferty's CP was yelling for artillery support. The troops coming out of Tarlac had opened fire on us. O'Day cut in again. The chief of staff, Major Villaluz, had just returned from the front and had positively identified the troops as the

13th Infantry. I switched through to our liaison officer and ordered fire, which opened promptly just before the enemy reached the stream in our front.

Just then five tanks and two SPMs broke out of Tarlac and came at high speed down the Manila North road, dispersing the troops to both sides, firing at them, and receiving fire. After some initial confusion, Hendry reported them as American. They fought their way to the stream and the blown-out bridge and moved up and down looking for a place to cross as Hendry covered them. They turned, started back toward Tarlac, met a hail of mortar fire, and returned to the bridge. The crews abandoned the vehicles and came into our lines on foot—with the exception of one crew, whose tank was hit and caught fire.

Late that night I saw Lieutenant Day at the Capas triangle. He had been in command of the SPM platoon with the tanks and told me the story. They had been operating near La Paz under 11th Division orders. Their withdrawal route to the south of La Paz having been cut off, they decided to gamble on reentering our lines at Tarlac. Near Tarlac they hit the rear of a large marching column of enemy troops. They took advantage of the surprise, dispersed the column, and fought their way into Tarlac. There they met heavy fire from troops in houses and behind walls and culverts. It was light caliber fire and didn't bother the tanks, but it played merry hell with Day's open-body half tracks.* Day told me of knocking over one machine gunner with his .45. He also reported seeing many Filipino civilians dead in Tarlac's streets.

The sad part was that the bridge that stopped them had been blown only a few hours before—after the order to withdraw to D-5 had been received, but several days later than the ordered time of destruction.

Hendry had no difficulty driving the enemy back into Tarlac, away from the tanks. Division organized a rescue party which was unsuccessful. Just before dark I received orders to destroy the abandoned vehicles by artillery fire. We dropped a

*The early SPMs were 75-mm. guns mounted on half-track chassis.—Ed.

lot of shells around them and got some hits, but darkness fell before destruction was complete.

Meantime, the action in front of the 21st Infantry and our 3rd Battalion had developed a lot of heat, as had the action on the extreme right of the 22nd Infantry. The pressure in front of the 22nd died down at dark, but the sound of heavy firing continued from the left flank, the bark of our guns dominating. I considered trying to get to the 3rd Battalion but decided against it. Except for giving moral support, I did not know what I could do after I got there. More important was last-minute news from the 11th Division of a tank and infantry attack down the axis of the La Paz–Magalang–Capas road, cutting into the marching flank of our division. It looked like a night fire action there. Assuming that the best thing was to get the bulk of the division safely out, I ordered Reed (Fisher's old battery) to that area, following the division shell as usual, and went myself. Harrison's Provisional Battery was already there. When I arrived, I was surprised to find Lieutenant Day and his remaining platoon plus a platoon of tanks. Day told me that elements of the 11th Division would retire down the road from La Paz, although that route was outside the division's area. This bitched things up to a fare-thee-well. It is one thing to have an antitank defense that can fire on anything moving in front of it. It is quite another to have to identify friend or foe first. Harrison had reported a brisk action in his front a short time before.

December 30 to 31. We called for volunteers—sacrifice men —to take positions at intervals for several kilometers down the road adjoining the area. We hoped, through their use of pre-arranged flashlight signals, to get a tipoff of hostile movement in time to fire. I coordinated the defense of the guns and tanks and then went to the Capas triangle to await developments.

Infantry began sifting through on both roads in buses and trucks and on foot. I was encouraged that they were in good shape and their units cohesive. Finally, after hours of waiting, came the rumble of our wooden-wheeled battalion, safely on its way to D-5. Mercado checked in and told me that when he pulled away from San Miguel after 8 P.M., he could still hear the 3rd Battalion firing, long after the scheduled hour of withdrawal.

A long interval and then came Valdez with the battalion, Hendry at the rear of the column pushing the "cripples" along ahead of him. By this time our civilian motor transport had developed many cripples. We repaired the vehicles when possible—without mechanics, tools, or parts—or doubled up loads and pushed the dead ones off a bridge or into a ditch. Savoie was still firing when Hendry pulled out.

I was exasperated at the Filipino habit of flipping the car headlights on and off every few hundred yards or so. The road was perfectly marked for miles by these flashing pinpoints. I told Sergeant Crabbe of Day's battery to smash the headlights of the next offender. Firing developed in Harrison's front and I went there. The firing subsided and I returned. Crabbe had bagged himself the car lights of the division commander, a couple of staff officers, and a regimental commander. I do not know if Crabbe ever shot anything with his pistol, but he did a fine job with its butt that night. The use of lights was inexcusable; there was bright moonlight, and a paper could be read anywhere on the road.

Finally the 21st Infantry began to filter back. They had been pretty roughly handled and told of heavy losses, but they were still in cohesive, small-unit formations. They had pulled back under cover of artillery fire.

Standing on the road and hearing the news of Acosta and Savoie's battalion, I had a feeling of pride and exultation. Win, lose, or draw, whether they escaped or lost all, they were doing the job for which God intended artillerymen magnificently— supporting the doughboy with the rifle.

Finally Reed came through and went into position with his SPM battery. He had withdrawn with the covering shell and had encountered no pressure on the Manila North road. The firing on the left had died down slowly and had finally stopped, but he could not guess the result of the action. The shell commander had decided, after action developed well to his right rear—possibly the same action we had in front of Harrison—to withdraw before dawn. We waited a seemingly interminable time—probably only about an hour. The division elements were apparently all behind us and on D-5. The 11th Division troops had stopped coming through hours before. Both the shell commander and the tank commander were anxious to get back to D-5 before dawn, not far away now.

I delayed as long as I could and was about to give the order when I heard the distant rumble of trucks and guns far down the road toward Tarlac. I knew exactly how Snitz Gruber felt when, with ear to the ground in that campaign on this same terrain more than forty years before, he heard the rumble of the caissons—the sound that inspired his shout, "I hear the caissons rolling," and later the field artillery song, "The Caissons Go Rolling Along."

Soon the battalion came along—the 3rd Battalion, 21st Field Artillery, Philippine Army; Lieutenant Acosta, the commander; Lieutenant Savoie, the American instructor—a battalion which that day had contributed gloriously to the annals of field artillery history. The men were tired, worn, and hungry, but cocky, proud, and aggressive. Standing there, Catalan and I were proud of them: every officer, man, truck, and gun.

I did not see Wappenstein that night, not until the middle of the Pio fire fight. There, Savoie was again doing a sweet job; and, well, I think I had better quote Wap's exact words:

"Mallonée, every man of the 21st Infantry who came out of Tarlac and the Bamban alive should get down on his knees and thank God for that red-headed son-of-a-bitch. He was everywhere he was needed at the right time. He held your guns in there by his personal example and damn near single-handed. He kept the guns in almost three hours after he could have withdrawn to give us a chance to break off. We were all out and the enemy knocked back into Tarlac before he pulled up a gun."

Later, Wappenstein recommended Savoie for the Distinguished Service Cross. On Bataan I had the pleasure of reading

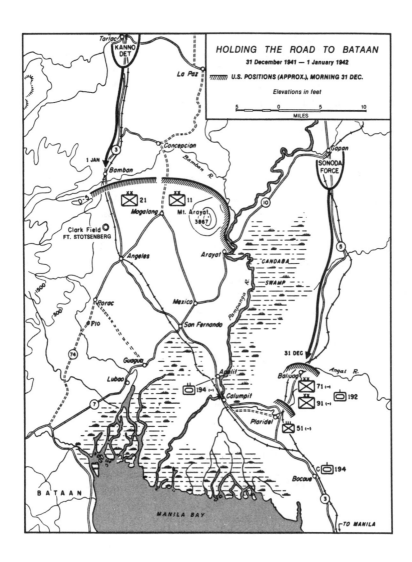

HOLDING THE ROAD TO BATAAN

31 December 1941 — 1 January 1942

////// U.S. POSITIONS (APPROX.), MORNING 31 DEC.

Elevations in feet

MILES

to Savoie the order conferring the cross on him. I hoped that when the relief expedition brought the actual cross, Wappenstein could pin it on Savoie. It was not to be. Colonel Wappenstein was killed during the final enemy drive against the Bataan force. Savoie was killed while a prisoner.

The order was given, the guns were moved out, and we were soon behind the D-5 line. Catalan and I arrived at our CP shortly before dawn. It was a turkey and chicken farm just outside Dau. That seemed to be its only advantage—the availability of food on the hoof. It was far from the division CP, which was completely out of touch with our battalions. It was in a perfect bombing triangle, with the junction of the Manila railroad and the Stotsenburg spur 100 yards away, the junction of the two similar highways another couple of hundred, and Clark Field and Camp Del Pilar in our backyard. I should have moved it, but I felt a strange fatalistic lethargy, and did not—besides, I was enjoying the eggs, chickens, and turkeys.

Tomas, my orderly, was sent home—finally. Bernado, my cook, and Jesus, the orderly for Harrison and Hendry, had enlisted, but Tomas was under age. I had ordered him out several times, but he wouldn't leave until we passed his home.

December 31. My new orderly, Datoon, had my bedding roll ready and I tumbled in. It started to rain and my restless sleep became very wet. I finally got up about 6:30 A.M. to find everything dry except my bed. The moral is: never pitch your bunk under bamboos on the edge of a stream. They weep.

Catalan and I gorged ourselves on eggs and then visited the battalions.

The D-5 line ran from the mountains (very close to the highway near us), along the high ground north of the Bamban River, crossed the river near a bridge, and continued to the east south of the river.

My concern was with our 1st Battalion. The Bamban River was practically dry, presenting no obstacle at all to infantry and not a serious one to vehicles. In front of the 1st Battalion were wide fields of uncut sugar cane, limiting the infantry field of fire and giving the enemy excellent covered routes of approach out of view of artillery observers. The 1st Battalion guns were in another of these damned rat-trap positions. There were no roads to the rear; the only route of withdrawal was one road paralleling the front line.

The 2nd Battalion was near a hacienda overlooking the Bamban, east of Mabalacat. The 3rd Battalion was on the Stotsenburg backroad near Dolores. This was all familiar territory to me and gave me many heartaches of recollection: Aguinaldo's Nose, the Sugar Loaf, Storm King Mountain, Third River, the Forage Farm. The fern-laden trail up to the Knifeedge especially used to delight my wife as we rode on horseback underneath arches of cogon grass higher than our heads, through Fern Canyon, and back to the post. Those were happy days, but this day I was not happy.

The next day Catalan and I went to see the damage done to Clark Field and Stotsenburg by the enemy air attack. We went past Dolores and entered Stotsenburg by the back road. We had been notified that Fort Stotsenburg had been abandoned, and if there was anything there we wanted, it was ours for the asking. Our supply officer had gone there and returned with a black eye, a truckload of canned goods, a case of butter, and a truckload of blankets. He got the black eye from a cavalry officer who accused him of looting and wanted me to have him shot. The personal effects of the cavalry officers also had been abandoned by the post people, and the cavalry officer drew a fine line between taking abandoned personal effects and abandoned government property. Fortunately, our supply officer was in the clear, for he had nothing but government property on his trucks.

Stotsenburg was a ghost town. Not a living thing could be seen. It reminded me of deserted Nevada and Arizona mining towns. The quarters I had occupied so happily a few years before and so uneasily a few weeks earlier were boarded up. I felt a chill through my heart—like looking at the face of a friend suddenly dead. The parade ground was high in grass and strangely unfamiliar. I had passed the flagpole hundreds of times, but, except at retreat formations, I doubt if I had ever consciously noted the flag. Now the pole looked naked and ashamed, resembling a captured maiden stripped bare on the auction block of a barbarian market. I saw no bomb damage in the quarters or administrative part of the post—only the desolation of abandoned disaster.

Clark Field was a sickening sight. Blackened, twisted, burned, shapeless masses of metal junk. Carcasses of what had been sleek racehorses of the air: the thoroughbred pursuits, the P-40s, the disdainful draft Percherons and Clydesdales, the B-17s. Most were lined up on the apron where they had been awaiting the return of their crews from the ill-fated lunch. A few were in the hangars, others in camouflaged positions around the field's edge.

Heartsick and despondent, I felt a sense of failure and disaster. I had hoped against hope that our damage was slight, that our air power was being conserved for the critical days on Bataan. Now I knew this hope was futile. We would continue to be pinned to the ground, our daylight movement paralyzed, bombed at will, until a new air force arrived from the States.

I had heard many reasons given for the Clark Field disaster, ranging from bad luck to criminal negligence. The reason was spilled milk—what was positive and vital was the fact of the destruction.*

We drove around the field counting the skeletons. There were more than thirty, including thirteen B-17s and B-18s. Suddenly the command car driver let out a yell. Herman and

---

*The reason remains as obscure today as it did to the author in 1942. No satisfactory explanation has ever been given as to why the planes were caught on the ground hours after hostilities had started.—Ed.

eight of his companions were heading for us and coming fast. We were in the middle of the runway with not even a blade of grass for cover. The driver stepped on the gas and we made the woods a split second before three planes dropped out of formation and came for us. We found a nice V Trench and dove for cover. The planes looked us over for several minutes and then went about their business, and so did we.

The line was fairly quiet on New Year's Eve. We had a mild celebration at the CP, although what we had to celebrate was not too evident. At midnight we opened a bottle of a very mild sweet effervescent wine—a poor substitute for champagne. I thought of my beloved wife and our long-standing custom of slipping away from the party as soon as possible after midnight and splitting a bottle of champagne in thanks for the happy past year and with a prayer for continued happiness.

The line remained quiet on New Year's Day. Personally, the day was very pleasant for me. General Weaver and his aide made a special trip to my CP to bring the news of my promotion and to swear me in. I made out the oath of office, swore to it before the aide, Captain Pettie, as summary court, and so became on January 1, 1942, a colonel of field artillery. My rank dated from December 19, 1941, but I could understand the delay in transmitting the order. We had some canned milk, plenty of eggs, and a carefully saved bottle of rye, so I mixed some eggnog in double celebration of New Year's Day and my promotion. Then it was time to get set for the next withdrawal.

We started the withdrawal from the D-5 line at 7 P.M. January 1. The South Luzon Force had passed behind our right wing, and division told us the night's movement would complete the folding back of the 71st and 91st Divisions. We would thus have two divisions, the 11th and the 21st, covering the entire army front, facing an aggressive hostile force estimated at 120,000 men.

No news from the front or from division had reached us after 2 P.M. There were no sounds of firing, and my mind was at ease. If I had known what was actually happening, I would have been frantic. I cannot imagine how the sounds of firing were so deadened that I could not hear them, nor why news of the late afternoon engagement did not get to us from division. Actually, an engagement like that at Tarlac was being repeated on the Bamban—severe late afternoon pressure on the left flank and on the North road. From the reports I received that night and later, the part played by the artillery was as decisive as at Tarlac.

Catalan and I checked the column past us south of Angeles, after having been to Day's position east of Angeles and to Harrison's south of Angeles on the Manila road. The area around the Angeles station was in flames.

Bonner and Villa-Real reported during the afternoon that our CP had been selected at San Jose, about 3,000 yards behind our battalions; division CP was at Pabanlag, the hacienda of Speaker Yulo of the Philippine legislature, who had just been elected senator. This hacienda was a couple of miles to our rear, but the selection had been approved by division.

I saw Major McLaughlin on the road south of Porac. He was very congratulatory about the work done by Filipino Lieutenant Corleto and Battery E. He said the battery's fire destroyed a wooden bridge while Japanese tanks were crossing, dropping eight vehicles into the river.

When Catalan and I arrived at San Jose, we found that division had changed its mind and had preempted our CP location. In addition, the 26th Cavalry and a tank battalion had located there. The town was as full as the county seat during fair week. Villa-Real, almost tearful in his exasperation, had nothing to offer except to locate us at Panbanlag, too far out of the picture. I accepted the situation that night and in the morning made a personal reconnaissance for a CP forward—and remained at Panbanlag. The country was flat canefield and, with the exception of San Jose, offered no shelter. San Jose was so obvious it invited bombing.

January 2 began quietly. I was not pleased with the gun positions from the standpoint of aerial protection, but what

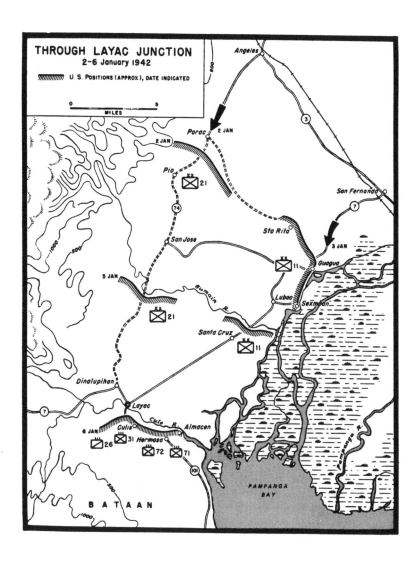

THROUGH LAYAC JUNCTION
2-6 January 1942

U. S. POSITIONS (APPROX.), DATE INDICATED

0   5
MILES

the hell could be done on the top of a billiard table, I didn't know. The left flank was still held by Wappenstein's 21st Infantry, which was actually pretty well used up by the engagements at Villasis, Tarlac, and the Bamban plus the almost constant pressure since December 24. The 26th Cavalry was now patrolling from our left flank into the Zambales.

As soon as Battery E rejoined, I ordered Mercado of the 2nd Battalion to reconnoiter positions nearer the center for occupation that night. After talking to Warren, Wappenstein's executive instructor, and hearing the extent of the 21st Infantry's losses and that it had 100 men for each kilometer of front, I decided to leave the guns behind that flank. McCafferty, on the right, was better off.

The enemy followed us closely and delivered another afternoon attack. Again the left flank was their objective. The 21st resisted stubbornly but was slowly forced back to the vicinity of Pio. The attack finally was stopped, but the line could not be restored.

Savoie and Harrison recommended to me that the guns withdraw during the night. The action had died down when I went over the gun positions with them. I thought they were joking when they pointed out the line on which the enemy had been stopped—about as far from the muzzles as outfielders would play for Babe Ruth if there were no fences.

Positions were available about six hundred yards to the rear and had the advantage of a close observation post that looked directly down the axis of the Pio ravine, from which the hostile line faced our refused left flank. The guns of the left battalion would have a partial enfilade fire down that ravine. I gave the order to withdraw to the rearward position during the night of January 2 to 3. The division plan was altered during that night, North Luzon Force ordering one battalion of the 23rd held for force reserve. Accordingly, the 2nd Battalion of the 23rd Infantry was designated to move up at dawn and restore the line on the left.

On the morning of January 3 I telephoned Acosta and Harrison, who reported no hostile activity. I went with Bonner to the right of the line, but then heavy firing developed on the left, and we got over there as fast as we could. The enemy had, in fact, beaten the 23rd to the punch. As the 23rd advanced, it was met by a withering fire, lost heavily, and did not restore the line.

As Bonner and I arrived, the line was coming slowly back. The CO of the attack battalion had been hit, and his body was being loaded into an ambulance-bus together with many others just as Herman and two companions strafed the road from no more than 150 feet. Bonner and I found a nice culvert, but the wounded in and around the bus were not so fortunate.

The line finally held but well on our side of the Pio ravine. Bonner and I stayed until the firing died down, then visited Wappenstein just as he finished a conference with his officer instructors—a dejected and disheartened group. They had been constantly engaged since Tarlac and were tired, hungry, and badly in need of sleep. Several had wounds. Their units were badly reduced in strength, almost to the point of ineffectiveness. But they returned to their units willingly—and grimly—to do the best they could.

I went back to the division CP to find out what the plan was for the left of the line. On the way I passed Colonel Maher, the chief of staff, who had visited our gun positions. Later he commented to me upon the excellence of the gun crews, saying the guns were being served as coolly and calmly as if it were peacetime practice.

There had been no Japanese artillery in action at Tarlac and the Bamban except the small infantry pack gun, a fine light weapon used for close-range direct support, handling effectively, however, most of the close-in missions for which we normally employed divisional artillery. After Porac it was different. Hostile artillery pounded the line and the rear areas, especially the latter. We had our first taste of the much-heralded Japanese 105-mm., and I will say I did not like the receiving end one damn bit. At Pio and Porac, however, the enemy artillery fire was not particularly effective.

At division I was surprised to find it was still the middle of the morning, so much had happened. We went over the situation, and the division commander decided to hold where he was, reorganizing the 2nd Battalion of the 23rd and reestablishing the line with it by local attacks as the situation permitted.

At 11 A.M. I was about to start to Panbanlag when Savoie called me to report all hell had broken loose. The enemy was coming out of Porac and Pio like bees out of a swarm, and the line was crumbling on the left. From then on reports came thick and fast. Within an hour the reserve line was disintegrating. By noon there was no organized line on the left flank at all. One battalion of the 21st in the division center still had some cohesion but had dropped back to conform to the left. There was a gap between the 21st and the 22nd, and the enemy threw a strong force into it.

I went to see what, if anything, we could do.

During this action, the 21st Field Artillery wrote a glorious page of history for itself. The 1st Battalion on the right swung its fire to the left front and fired at ranges of six hundred to eight hundred yards using shrapnel shell* set at site zero and range zero, effectively limiting the hostile penetration in the center. The 2nd and 3rd Battalions, with their enfilade fire up the Pio ravine, caught a tank group assembling to attack. A two-battalion concentration of massed fire was placed on these tanks, sixteen guns firing eight rounds per gun minute. A few tanks and trucks got out toward Porac but none crossed the

---

*A round of ammunition containing steel balls last used extensively in anger in WWI. This may be the only example of their use as late as WWII. "Schrapnel" used in present-day war dispatches is a distinct misnomer and really means "shell fragments."—Ed.

crest in our direction. A staff officer from North Luzon Force submitted a report giving us official credit for twenty tanks. Wave after wave of enemy troops came on and were beaten back. Our own line evaporated. For six hours the muzzles of our guns were the most advanced element of the 21st Division on the left of the line. The North Luzon Force intelligence summary for the day told of the artillery battalions repulsing infantry attacks at point-blank range.

There was nothing I could do but cheer them on. It was suicide to attempt a withdrawal under small arms fire during daylight, and it looked like sure capture to stay on without infantry support. The division was in bad shape. Only our guns were holding together the bones of a meatless skeleton. To withdraw the guns would have, without question, collapsed the division, and with it possibly the entire force.

As attack after attack came on, broke, and went back, I knew what Cushing's artillerymen must have felt, with the muzzles of their guns in the front line, as the Confederate wave came and broke on the high-water mark at Gettysburg.

I kept waiting for the division reserve, which did not come. Finally, after determining that Savoie, Acosta, Mercado, and Harrison knew how to blow up their guns, I went back to division to find out about the reserve.

As I left, I had serious doubts that I would ever see those fine young men again. I had a sense of cowardice in leaving them there, but since I had contributed as much as I could toward their morale and there was nothing tactical or technical that I could do for them up forward, I might do something to get aid to them by going to the rear.

On the way back I saw Wappenstein and Warren at a new CP in a ditch between the road and a canefield. They had been shot out of the old CP and, as Wap expressed it, his CP was in his hat.

At division the situation was known and the reserve had been alerted, but no orders had gone to it because the general was loath to commit the last reserve until it was imperative. I suggested that the situation be radioed to force and that permission be requested to move up the battalion of the 23rd held as a force reserve. This was granted in a very short time, but in the meantime Savoie and Harrison continued to call in the reports on the action. The enemy was still coming and still going back. Finally both battalions of the 23rd were ordered up to counterattack and restore the line.

As soon as I heard the order, I relayed the news to our battalion CP, located at the observation post commanding the Pio ravine, and heard loud cheers from the personnel around the phone at the other end.

Then there was what seemed an interminable delay. Both battalions of the 23rd had been alerted long since and should have moved immediately. General Capinpin became exasperated and had Bobby Tuason phone twice with insistent orders to get moving. Finally he lost his temper, and the CP spewed out staff officers to build a fire under the 23rd.

There was no hostile infantry action during this long delay, but our battalion observation post was catching hell from hostile artillery. The enemy apparently concluded that we were on the ridge, and ranged on us. But their adjustment was about one hundred yards over and, beyond shortening the space between the ears and shoulder blades of my young men, the fire had no effect.

Then Savoie reported small hostile patrols feeling their way around to the left and rear of the CP, and the biggest attack of the afternoon started. From the observation post they took turns telling me about it. In the last war I was an active participant. Here I felt like a bystander. Finally they reported that the advance wave of the 23rd had reached about two hundred yards behind them, and then the telephone went dead. The line wasn't out; the phone was still "live," but I could get no answer from the other end. After ten or fifteen minutes of hellish worry, Savoie's jubilant voice reported that the enemy's most powerful attack of the day had culminated in a mass drive down the ravine toward the extreme left flank. The artillery fire withered it and drove it back, and it was all over.

The 23rd was arriving on the line of the guns but it was not advancing farther, despite the fact that there wasn't an enemy soldier in sight and not a shot was being fired. About this time the division staff officers returned, reporting a successful counterattack and the restoration of the line. This was radioed to force and elicited a congratulatory reply. The congratulations were well deserved. The division had met and repulsed severe attacks and retained its cohesion.

By dark the situation was still quiet. It was Bonner and Catalan's trick at the forward CP, so I went to Pabanlag for a shower and dinner. I turned in and had slept an hour or two when the telephone operator, who invariably was at my bedside during the night, awakened me. I picked up the phone to hear Harrison, usually calm and collected, in a near panic. The infantry had not gone ahead of the guns but instead had consolidated a line about two hundred yards to the rear. Our gun positions and observation post were receiving a brisk rifle fire from the flanks and rear. Harrison believed a hostile force had made a night attack from the flank against the infantry and had hit behind the line of guns. Savoie was not there and he, Harrison, had decided to blow the guns and try to fight a way out with the men.

Whether it was sleep, weariness, or just slow mental processes, I was off base and stuttering mentally. I have no idea what I would have told him, but at that moment Bonner's cool and rather amused voice cut in. He had the news and reports of the division CP and correctly estimated the situation. Actually, the rear elements of the reserve had finally gotten up and had bumped into some jittery units already up; in the confusion, firing started—but there were no Japanese troops there. Harrison and the battalions sat tight, close to the ground, and in a few minutes it was all over.

The incident cost us one killed, four wounded, and nine missing in action. Those missing were believed to have been killed or wounded in canefield fires started by the shooting. As a result of the action, the North Luzon Force summary for January 3 credited the 21st Field Artillery with having saved the day for the division.

During the night of January 2 to 3, the enemy had moved up some 105-mm. guns, whose long range caused us considerable annoyance but not much danger. The most irritating thing was that they had slipped one or possibly two guns of fairly heavy caliber around our left flank or through one of the gaps to a position several thousand yards behind our left flank among the foothills of the Zambales, thereby commanding a view of our entire rear area. This fire almost paralyzed traffic in our rear areas, sniping at trucks, cars, and even individuals.

Although the 4th was quiet for us, it was a busy day for the 11th Division. A tank platoon radio kept us informed of the situation there, which deteriorated as the hours passed. Finally the tank radio told us the division line had "evaporated"—the term the operator used. A large infantry force had been cut off from the 11th Division route of withdrawal and was marching into the 21st Division area in an attempt to get around the enemy and reestablish itself between the hostile force and Dinilupihan. This pullout threw McCafferty's right completely in the air and cluttered up the already insufficient route of withdrawal available to him.

I went to that flank and spent a portion of the afternoon there waiting for something to happen, but, except for a few half-hearted feelers, it was quiet. I returned to the division CP to find that orders for withdrawal at 7 P.M. had been received late in the afternoon.

The bridge at Pabanlag was interdicted during this withdrawal, but it was well defiladed and we had no casualties.

Reed covered the rear, moving by bounds, and I followed the tail of the column after it passed me.

I had been very dissatisfied with the CPs selected during the withdrawals. Without exception, they had been too far to the rear and in prominent houses inviting bombing or shelling. Their occupation was never smooth and orderly: confusion reigned; trucks stood on the road; officers evinced no interest in anything except their own comfort. After commenting about these matters informally many times, I finally called a staff meeting during a lull at Pabanlag and emphasized what should be done.

I thought that this ironed out the matter, but when I arrived at the new CP, I found things even worse than usual. The CP was in the only barrio for miles around, and about as far from the battalions as it was possible to get without going into Dinalupihan. Instead of spreading installations over several hundred yards to minimize potential losses, the entire CP was less than fifty yards from one edge to another.

I regret that I lost my temper and told Catalan publicly in mule-skinner language that the position violated every known consideration of CP selection or organization, and that if it was the best that his staff, including Villa-Real, could do after so many similar failures had been repeatedly pointed out, I would recommend that he clean out the stable and start afresh with a staff that could secure results.

Catalan became very formal and defended Villa-Real and the staff by saying that the CP would move anywhere I desired, and that the staff would await my orders. This attempt at lip service to my wishes, when it was obvious I could not give any reasonable command in pitch-dark territory I had never seen even in daylight, infuriated me. I told him to leave his rear echelon where it was to be blown to hell, to load his command echelon in cars, and to return to the vicinity of the gun positions where we would wait the night out, making suitable reconnaissance and establishing the CP in daylight.

Villa-Real then remembered that there was a suitable place for another look-see; Catalan and I surveyed the surrounding area in the dark.

When Villa-Real returned, he ignored me completely and made a very formal report to Catalan. "Sir, the regimental executive of the 21st Field Artillery of the Philippine Army presents his respects to the commanding officer of the 21st Field Artillery of the Philippine Army and reports that a suitable location for the regimental command post has been selected and is being established by the staff."

Later, I could see that I accomplished no good purpose by blowing up. The staff had not been relieved nor could it be, and I had antagonized its officers, especially Villa-Real. I regretted this, for he was a keen, enthusiastic youngster who, with training and experience, could develop into an excellent officer. It was not his fault that the paucity of officers of rank and experience in the Philippine army resulted in his elevation to a position of responsibility far beyond his years. His mistakes were no more glaring than those of a young American officer of similar age, background, and training. I was fond of him personally, and with an American officer the incident would have passed off as discipline. But with him I was afraid the hurt to his pride could never be overcome.*

Early on January 5 Catalan and I went to the battalions. For very good reason the proud fighting spirit of the preceding three days had vanished. The battalions were close together, almost in close bivouac formation. There were no foxholes, trenches, or other means of protecting guns, men, or fire-direction centers. Worse, no one seemed to give a damn and no one was doing anything. While we were there, Colonel O'Day arrived, and together we received news via the tank

---

*Upon reading this in 1971, Villa-Real commented, "Wrong. Colonel Mallonée and I had our professional differences, but they did not affect our personal relations."—Ed.

radio. The situation in front of the 11th Division was bad. It had retired and was in a state aptly expressed by the word "fluid." We were completely out of contact with it on our right flank. We had no pressure on our front—thank God, because the infantry, as far as I could see, and certainly the artillery, were incapable of offering even feeble resistance.

We were in serious danger of being outflanked on our right and cut off from the bottleneck entrance to Bataan if the enemy drove a wedge across the road between our rear and the Layac junction bridge, denying us that sole route of withdrawal.

I agreed with O'Day there was no prospect of using our guns in that position, and that it would be more effective to move them south of the river to positions from which they could fire in advance of the junctions of the roads from Dinalupihan to Layac and from Guagua to Layac—the bottleneck through which we all had to enter Bataan.

O'Day recommended that I order this withdrawal, but I declined the responsibility because such a move was not merely a change of position, but a change of mission. Leaving the situation as it was, I went back to Dinalupihan with Catalan to see the division commander.

En route we saw Wappenstein, who gave me a copy of a message from Capinpin. It was ambiguous, but Wappenstein explained it to mean that the infantry would withdraw to conform to the line of the 11th Division, the artillery doing likewise. The position to be occupied was designated as "the hills to your rear." Since we were in flat cane country, and the only hills to the rear were across the river in Bataan, this was so indefinite that we continued on to the division CP for clarification.

As we got there, General Capinpin rushed up, waving his arms excitedly. I did not have any opportunity to tell him O'Day's advice, for he began shouting at us while we were getting out of the car. His orders were not entirely in accord with my feelings, and for that reason, I entered them in my note-book as soon as we left him. In view of subsequent develop-ments, I doubt if I will ever forget them.

"Get out. Get out. Get the guns out."

"Very well, sir. Where shall we go?"

"Anywhere into Bataan. Get across the bridge. Get south of Hermosa, find a place and bivouac. I will find you tomorrow."

"Do you mean we are through here, sir, that you do not want any further artillery support of the division?"

"Are you firing? Are we in contact?"

"No, sir, and very little prospect today."

"Then get across the river. Things are bad on our right. The 11th Division has fallen to pieces. We will probably all be cut off. The infantry can get out by swimming the river, but the guns will be lost. Get out. Hurry."

"Shouldn't I go into position just south of the river so as to fire in front of the bridge and keep it open?"

"No. Get south of Hermosa."

We started back to effect this order, en route meeting Bon-ner. I was so disturbed by the thought of withdrawing, that I explained the situation to him and ordered him to go to the North Luzon Force CP and ask for assignment of a bivouac location in conformity to the division commander's order. I did not feel like going over Capinpin's head, but asking for a bivouac area would let them know about his order.

Bonner went to force, Catalan went to the guns to start the withdrawal, and I stayed near Dinalupihan and reconnoitered for gun positions—just in case. I selected tentative positions near Dinalupihan and returned to our CP. There with Catalan I checked the guns past us. We tailed the column into Dinalupi-han, where we met Bonner.

General Wainwright had strongly disapproved of the with-drawal. He ordered that the regiment continue its support of the division and gave Bonner a message to Capinpin directing that the division hold the line of the river south of Pabanlag, as per previous orders. As we knew, the division had already retired from that line to conform to the 11th Division. Catalan and I went to the division CP for new orders, but Capinpin was away.

Bonner, on his return trip from the force CP, had ordered each battalion commander to turn around and return to Dinalupihan, sending a staff officer in advance for orders. I placed each battalion in the area I had reconnoitered.

While the battalions were still moving south near Hermosa, the enemy bombed that town and bombed and strafed the column. It was the severest mass bombing we had yet received. An ammunition dump in Hermosa exploded and set the town on fire. Yet strangely enough, our column suffered no casualties or damage. After the bombing stopped, the regiment turned around and started back to the front. This must have been confusing to the hostile air observers.

Soon the guns arrived, and I went to the division CP to report the new situation and find out what was happening. Wainwright was there. He was telling Capinpin that the 21st Division was too anxious to withdraw, and that he—Wainwright—had found the artillery south of the bridge and had turned it around. The inference was that the artillery had pulled out on its own. I waited for Capinpin to explain, or at least to accept responsibility for the order, but he did neither. He told Wainwright the artillery had merely been changing position and had overrun the marker at the turnoff point. This was so improper that I saw red and stepped up to expostulate. Wainwright turned his back upon me and started to point out something on his map. I cooled down enough to realize that this was not the place for family bickerings, and backed off. Later Bonner told me that he had emphasized to Wainwright that the withdrawal order had been issued by Capinpin.

A few minutes later, Wainwright talked with Colonel O'Day while I was standing three feet away. He exhorted O'Day to continue efforts, patting him on the back and saying, "You are the only soldier I have in this division. You are the only one I can depend upon in the division, and you can't let me down."

Up to that moment I had been extremely proud of the record of my regiment, and of my own record. I felt that the regiment, despite many shortcomings, had functioned far in excess of reasonable expectations, that it was the backbone of the division and had prevented complete disintegration of the division many times. To have my regiment accused of cowardice and desertion and to receive such a personal slap in the official face was plenty tough. It hurt for a long time.

During the course of an otherwise uneventful afternoon, a tearful battery commander came to Colonel Catalan, and then both came to me. Savoie had slapped his face. We soothed him, much as I used to sooth my children—except that I didn't kiss the hurts—and then sent for Savoie. The red-headed boy was still mad and willing to throw up his job in disgust. He had visited the battery and found nothing done and nothing doing. After a protracted hunt, he had found the battery commander in a house amusing his officers by playing a guitar while they sang. He ventured a saucy reply to Savoie. This was too much for the fiery Louisianan, who jerked the officer to his feet and slapped him with an open hand, knocking him down. When he reached me, Savoie was in despair at getting effective results. He said that he had tried to be everywhere at once and keep things going. He got only lip service from the officers. I quieted him down and impressed him with the necessity of not fighting the battalion, despite all obstacles. I cautioned him again about his profanity and about manhandling any individual.

I know that, in the main, conditions were as Savoie represented. But, with the pill I had just swallowed, it was difficult to give him an admonition.

In the 2nd Battalion, Harrison, an impulsive, enthusiastic youngster, wept into my crying towel at regular intervals about the deficiencies of the officers. In the 1st Battalion, Hendry, a quiet, self-contained, mild-mannered individual, was handling most of the load himself, having despaired of getting assistance from officers or men. In headquarters, Bonner was thoroughly disgusted with the caliber of the staff and the ineptness of the communication personnel. All in all, it was a most unpleasant day.

Nothing developed during the afternoon. This time I got—by insistence—a written order for withdrawal.

The triangle at Layac junction was the exact center of the bottleneck, the fever spot of the entire withdrawal, the point at which vigorous enemy bombing would have the best chance of disrupting the entire operation.

At the triangle there shortly appeared General Capinpin's car, several staff cars, several cavalry cars, some regimental commander cars, a few 11th Division cars, and then some North Luzon Force cars. It looked like the parking lot of the Yale Bowl.

The 11th Division units began to pass through the bottleneck, and, at the same time, the 21st Division covering force arrived from Dinalupihan and turned north toward Guagua, making two solid columns of troops going in opposite directions. Finally the 11th Division reported clear, and the 21st Infantry was given the order to move into Bataan. Soon the covering force and the artillery were the sole remnants of the North Luzon Force outside the pearly gates of Bataan. I got the release order from Capinpin, directed Catalan to put his regiment in motion, turned over the command of the SPMs to Major Ganahl as ordered, reverted to the status of an instructor-adviser—without command but with responsibility—and at about midnight of January 5 to 6 followed the last gun of the 21st Field Artillery across the river into Bataan.

A great weight of responsibility slipped off my shoulders. I had been under far greater strain than I realized. I had brought a brand-new, babes-in-arms regiment from training camp to beach defense and from Lingayen Gulf to a withdrawal, which for many reasons is one of history's most remarkable retirements in the face of an enemy. The regiment had fulfilled its mission with distinction, even though the force commander was not sufficiently in possession of the facts to be aware of it. We had not lost a gun, and there had not been a gun withdrawn before the enemy except by order. More important, the infantry commanders were more than satisfied with the support we had given them—all this despite ill-trained officers and men, insufficient equipment, and inadequate material.

But now we were within the pearly gates; we were to have a few days rest behind the protection of the American and Scout units.

As we followed the last unit of the regiment across the bridge at Layac junction and into Bataan, the withdrawal phase ended, and the third and final phase of the Luzon campaign opened: the defense of the Bataan Peninsula. I knew Bataan from 1926 to 1929 as a jungle crossed by a few foot trails, even fewer pack trails, and no roads. Then, the defense of Bataan would have been mainly jungle fighting to impede enemy construction of roads which would permit siege artillery to be placed ready to fire on Corregidor. Except for the harbors near the south tip, which were under control of the Corregidor guns, there was only one harbor with water deep enough to allow the unloading of seagoing vessels. This was Subic Bay, defended by Fort Wint. Our engineers were convinced that, even discounting the delay our defensive forces might cause, the technical difficulties of road construction would not permit enemy action against Corregidor from Bataan within the time allotted before the arrival of a U.S. relief force.

When I arrived in the Philippines in 1941, I found this condition materially changed. A hard-surface road had been constructed from Subic Bay to Dinalupihan, where it joined another hard-surface road extending north to Guagua, San Fernando, and Manila, and south through Hermosa, Limay, and Lamac, to Mariveles on the tip of the peninsula. Another road crossed the northerly third of the peninsula east to west from Pilar to Bagac. Along the China Sea, or west side, was a nearly complete secondary road.

Thus, the virginity of the jungle had been broken to our military disadvantage. To offset this, I was told we had prepared defensive positions covering the roads and other critical areas; the jungle had been cleaned in front of these positions for excellent fields of fire; artillery positions had been created; and trails had been extended to the rear for supplies. Essentially, however, our defense was still based upon the impenetrability of the jungle.

In the one month less two days that had elapsed since the outbreak of war, it could not be expected that the defense measures would be complete. But I expected they would be adequate for the type of action foreseen, with initial essentials such as small arms fields of fire, planned artillery concentrations, infantry trenches, and antitank mine fields. This seemed a certainty when I realized that, in addition to 6,000 civilian workers, the Scout Division had been moved very early to Bataan together with one regular and two other divisions of the Philippine army and the entire supply services of USAFFE. Moreover, the American and Scout troops were the best-equipped, best-trained, and presumably the most reliable troops on Luzon.

Thus, I entered Bataan with a feeling of complacency. I envisioned a short rest period while our troops were reorganized and reequipped. I welcomed the breathing spell as an opportunity to weed out and replace officers of demonstrated weakness and inefficiency, and planned to come to a thorough understanding with Colonel Catalan about maintaining discipline.

I had a rude awakening. It took less than a day on Bataan to disillusion me. Trenches were nonexistent; individual foxholes had been dug after a fashion but were not connected laterally or to the rear. Barbed wire was so thin as to be classed as meager. Some artillery positions were dug in but without overhead protection, although it was obvious, after Clark Field, that the enemy would have complete air mastery. Supply trails to the front-line units in the jungle were inadequate. The jungle center of the line could not be supported by artillery because of the impossibility of pushing guns into the tangled growth.

This rude awakening was completed with a shock when, during the afternoon, news reached us that the enemy had followed closely upon our heels as we entered Bataan, hit the Layac junction defensive line with vigor at dawn, and cracked it, driving our best troops back onto the Mt. Natib line. The 23rd Field Artillery Battalion of the Scouts had been overrun when the infantry gave way; it lost its guns and ceased to exist as an organized unit.

The line was reformed on the north slope of Mt. Natib. It extended from Manila Bay north of Abucay, across the front of the Abucay hacienda, then across the north slope of the mountain to join the right flank of I Corps, and then to the China Sea.

Since the North and South Luzon Forces no longer existed as units after they entered Bataan, the I Corps was formed under the command of Major General Wainwright, who had as a staff the officers of the old North Luzon Force. The II Corps was under the command of Maj. Gen. George Parker. He had commanded the South Luzon Force until the early days of the war, when he had been sent to command the Bataan Defense Force, charged with the defense of the peninsula until the withdrawal was completed and with the preparation of Bataan for its defense.

The South Defense Force, which later became the Service Command, was under Brig. Gen. Allen MacBride, who had been chief of staff of the Philippine Department before the war.

The II Corps on the right had the 11th, 21st, and 41st Divisions and part of the Philippine Division. The 2nd Division, which was on beach defense of Manila Bay, overlapped the sector of II Corps and the Service Command. During the early days the 31st Division was transferred from I Corps to II Corps, and upon withdrawal from the Abucay line, the 11th Division was transferred from II Corps to I Corps. The 26th Cavalry was in USAFFE reserve.

Division organization, however, was not strictly adhered to on Bataan, being replaced by sector combat teams formed from divisional units.

The air corps ground troops, no longer needed for their normal function, were formed into an infantry combat unit.

USAFFE, under General MacArthur, commanded the whole from Corregidor, with an advance echelon of the general staff on Bataan. After MacArthur went to Australia, the USAFFE became USFIP (United States Forces in the Philippines) commanded by General Wainwright from Corregidor. All the forces on Bataan were constituted into the Luzon Force, U.S.A., under command of Maj. Gen. Edward King, who had been artillery adviser on MacArthur's staff. These changes of command took place between March 15 and 21.

During the morning of January 6 I took stock of the situation. I recalled the numerical strength of the enemy army and its high degree of training, polished by long years of campaigning in China and Siberia. I calculated the strength of that army's air corps, ably supported by the Japanese navy and naval air force. I gave full credit to Japanese control of the offensive, which enabled them to use containing forces on several of the Southeast Asia fronts while concentrating their major strength on a front of their own selection. Then I envisioned the deficiencies of the Philippine army—deficiencies for which no blame can be attached. On the contrary, the blame and shame must be largely borne by our own nation. It was an army with untrained personnel, inadequate equipment, inexperienced leadership, and antiquated weapons. In short, it was an army on paper; actually, an organized mob. To my mind it was marvelous that this army had offered any resistance at all.

The bivouac area of the 21st Division was at Guitol near Balanga. It was badly overcrowded—inadequate even for a regiment—had little natural cover, and was interspersed with thickets impossible for vehicles to penetrate. Infantry, artillery, and headquarters units were intermingled. All installations remained where they dropped the first night. Vehicles moved about at will; in one instance, a division motor-pool mechanic drove a car into our CP area, parked in the open, and calmly proceeded to do some repair work. My orders to him met a surly response, so I borrowed Bonner's pistol. At my count of seven, the car left on two wheels, with three seconds to spare.

At my insistence, our regiment did some desultory digging, but it took three days to get half-baked V trenches for the CP personnel. Inertia gripped all ranks. Sanitation was ghastly. Straddle trenches, when dug at all, adjoined kitchens. This was not as bad as it sounds, for the trenches were only a perfunctory gesture; calls of nature were answered when and where heard.

Food cans were dropped where they were emptied, and in a day or so the area was well carpeted with shiny, smelly sardine and salmon cans. I asked the division medical instructor in all seriousness how long it would be before an epidemic of intestinal disorders would hit. In all seriousness he answered, "One month." He was conservative by about two weeks.

Initially, this confusion and disorganization stemmed from the breakdown of a guide system to lead us into the bivouac area. But it continued, apparently to the complete contentment of the division staff.

During our first day at Guitol, I received a memorandum that had a far-reaching effect on the defense of Bataan. The condition necessitating the memorandum was the principal cause of the ultimate surrender—the most important single factor of the campaign, not even excluding the destruction of our air force.

The memorandum stated that the troops on Bataan would be on half-rations "temporarily." The ration components were listed as:

Rations for One for One Day

3.7 ounces of rice

1.8 ounces of sugar

1.2 ounces of canned milk

2.44 ounces of canned fish, salmon or sardines

Tomatoes when available, basis: ten men per can.

This ration—not even approaching a "half" ration—continued from January 6 until about the middle of February. For a short period bread was issued—memory says about two weeks. During the latter part of February, the rice ration went up to eight ounces, and during the last two weeks in March, to twelve ounces. Just before the end we got sixteen ounces. The canned fish was increased slightly to about six men per can. Three times during the campaign my regiment was issued carabao. We had carabao meat several other times, not issued but killed on the line and "procured." By the same method, we had calesa pony once and mule twice. I can recommend mule. There was little to choose between calesa pony and carabao. The pony was tougher but better flavored than the carabao. Iguana was fair. Monkey I do not recommend. I saw the hand of one cooked monkey and never got over it. I never had snake.

Personally, I was probably better off than most. I had purchased, before leaving Dagupan, about a case and a half of mixed canned goods: baked beans, corned beef hash, and vegetables. I supplemented this with about another half case when coming through Stotsenburg. I parceled out these rations to my officers in limited quantities, and we probably had just a shade more food than most others. Even so, I had to do a tailoring job on my waistband twice during the Bataan campaign.

The insufficiency of supplies other than food naturally affected the campaign. But the shortage of food was critical. Each day's output of energy in combat took its toll of the human body—a toll that could not be replenished from the energy furnished by the ironically termed half-ration.

Adequate food stocks existed in the islands, and one month's time should have been more than ample to move them to Bataan and Corregidor. The reason for not doing so seemed twofold. First, supplying troops at the beaches from stocks on Bataan would have been difficult because there was no railroad, and only one highway running from the peninsula. Second, and far more important, was the abandonment at the start of the war of WPO No. 3 and the decision instead to conduct an all-out defense at the beaches. This left the defense of

Bataan very insecure; it was possible to envision a Japanese landing in force on the peninsula while our army was on the beaches. Thus, it was conceivable that if Bataan were stocked, the stocks would be captured. When the decision was made— or forced upon the high command—to reinstitute WPO No. 3 and defend Bataan, only about one week's time was available to transfer food.

The sad fact is that we actually did abandon large stores of food to the enemy in Bataan and on Corregidor—stores that had been conserved too long.

While the regiment was in the Guitol area, orders were received promoting Hendry and Savoie to captain and Harrison to first lieutenant. None of the Filipino officers had been promoted. I sensed resentment. Investigating, I found that recommendations had been passed to the headquarters of the Philippine army for approval and were held up there. I suggested to Colonel Catalan that he could do more with his own people than I could. He tried, but without success. He told me some recommendations had failed to meet President Quezon's approval, resulting in all of them being suspended while the matter was ironed out.

I also recommended Major Bonner for promotion to lieutenant colonel, but his name was not on the promotion order. I found that, as a result of "policy," he had not been promoted because there was no specific table of organization rank for the duty he was performing—assistant to the senior instructor.

News from the front was not good. After the Layac junction line fell, the Japanese continued to press vigorously down the axis of the East road. Our front line was constantly under pressure, and frequent local counterattacks were necessary to maintain the position. As I expected, the failure of the enemy to drive down the East road caused an extension of action westward into the jungle along the front of Mt. Natib.

My short contact with Japanese maneuvering left me with no doubt about their ability to climb mountains and penetrate jungles, and I had an uneasy suspicion that we would consider the Mt. Natib jungle an adequate natural barrier. I talked with Major Kerr, one of II Corps' assistant G-3s. He was concerned only with the tidewater flats and was smugly complacent about the security of the corps left and the army center. He didn't know whether the flanks of the two corps were actually in contact, but he wasn't in the least alarmed if they were not. I also talked with Major Maury, S-3 of the Scout Artillery. He was visibly amused at my concern and told me there was a ravine across the front "sixty feet deep" and almost vertical, and that "the enemy will have to have a brigade of human flies" to cross that barrier and gain access to our jungle flank.

The attack that broke the hacienda–Mt. Natib position came directly across Maury's uncrossable ravine. On the night of January 9, after three days' rest and on less than one hour's notice, my regiment went back into action. The 3rd Battalion went into position near the Abucay hacienda in general support of the front line, subject to calls for reinforcing fire from the Scout Artillery. The 1st Battalion occupied a position southeast of Abucay with the primary mission of beach defense, and the 2nd Battalion went north of Balanga with the same mission. The regimental CP remained at Guitol until the 12th. There was some confusion as to our status. We were relieved from the 21st Division—and were never again with it— but we had not been attached elsewhere.

While I was at Guitol and still under the 21st, General Capinpin very formally presented me with a copy of a letter he was submitting, recommending me for the Distinguished Service Medal for my service during the withdrawal. I learned later that the letter was returned to Capinpin with instructions to resubmit it at the end of the campaign, since it was not policy to make such awards during the course of action. I favored this policy and had no criticism.

On January 12 orders were received attaching the 21st Field Artillery (less its 3rd Battalion) to the 11th Division, which was charged with the beach defense of Manila Bay. Our 3rd Battalion was attached to the Scout Artillery. Catalan, Bonner, and I reported to General Brougher, commanding the 11th. The general was indefinite in his orders, merely saying that Lieutenant Colonel Hughes, commanding the 11th Field Artillery, would coordinate the artillery for beach defense.

I spent several days going over the beach and our dispositions for defense. There was considerable beach and a paucity of defense. Hughes had only ten guns in his regiment organized into one four-gun and three two-gun batteries. He planned to stand back from the beach and use indirect fire. Not only did I doubt that the officers in my regiment and Hughes's could efficiently handle indirect fire against moving targets even in daytime, but the telephone wire necessary to provide the communications net required for this type of action was insufficient. This clearly indicated that the massing of artillery fire upon a specific zone would be impossible. A decentralization of artillery command was the only solution. Although loath to relinquish the advantages of massed fire, I started to organize the 21st Field Artillery for beach defense based upon decentralization.

I was not happy about our battalion positions. They were neither close enough to the water for direct fire nor far enough back for indirect fire. The best I could hope was that the guns could sweep the area between the muzzles and the beach after the enemy landed.

While at Brougher's CP for a conference, I had one of my two very narrow escapes of the campaign. Japanese planes were continuously bombing the temporary landing field along the Pilar-Bagac road, starting their dives from a point over the CP. Familiarity breeds contempt, and I was reading a news bulletin —the first one I had seen—when three planes took a dive at us. I also took a dive—toward a trench. When the attack was over and I crawled out, there was a neat machine-gun hole drilled through the papers I still clutched in my hand. Several men were killed or wounded.

Japanese planes began to take a toll of the regiment by this time. I do not believe they ever deliberately bombed any of

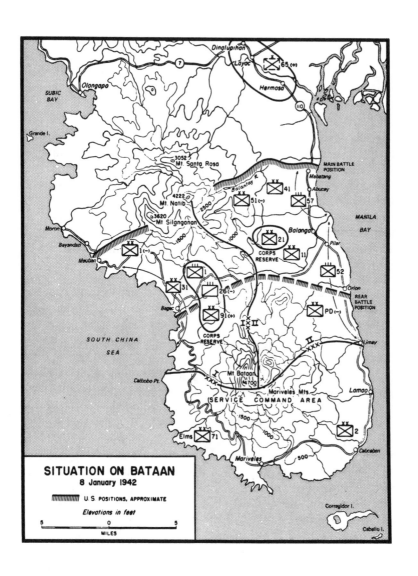

SITUATION ON BATAAN
8 January 1942

||||||||| U.S. POSITIONS, APPROXIMATE

Elevations in feet

5   0   5
MILES

our batteries, but we were located in the edges of barrios along
the East road that were bombed one by one from north to
south and in attacks that found our batteries. We lost several
men. One bomb scored a direct hit on an SPM battery ammunition truck. Three of our guns were damaged but not one was
put out of action. In fact, despite almost daily bombing and
shelling that left scars on every gun in the regiment, we had
only three guns put out of action during the entire campaign.
This can be attributed to three things: good fortune, dug-in
gun pits well sandbagged, and the fact that the Japanese never
poured in the volume of fire necessary for destruction. A few
bombs at a time from the plane was the rule. Similarly, their
artillery would adjust, obtain a bracket, and then fire eight to
twelve rounds at most. I concluded there was a shortage of
bombs and shells.

I continued to exhort greater efforts at protection, praising
here, condemning there. I was never satisfied. I believed that,
after the first men were killed, the object lesson would cause
the others to dig without my spur. Such was not the case. We
moved frequently either because our positions had been found
and bombed, or to prevent their being found and bombed. This
necessitated constant digging, and, as each day passed, the men
got weaker—and more fatalistic. I feel certain that if it had not
been for my insistent efforts, ably seconded by Colonel Catalan, many more men would have been killed. As it was, we lost
about twenty-five men killed and about fifty wounded. Until
the last few days, every man killed or seriously wounded had
been above ground, not in his trench. Men who hit their holes
fast enough came through unscathed or with minor injuries. We
had many instances of trenches caving in from near misses. If
the trenches were deep and the men were standing bent over,
they could scramble out or keep breathing until dug out. If the
trenches were shallow and the men prone in the bottom, they
were unconscious when dug out and needed resuscitation—
which failed in only two cases. As hunger weakened the men,
they honestly could not dig the trenches to the proper depth,

and the dig-out cases increased. Nevertheless, I am sure that my efforts in this direction saved many lives. Two officers and a detail were left at the new location; Lieutenant Malinit was to prepare the area for the battery section: kitchen, switchboard, first aid station, and personnel shelter; Lt. Antonio Aquino was to do the same for the command section, cutting about fifty feet of trail into the area in addition. Each was to post guides for vehicles.

Aquino was my favorite among the junior staff officers. The son of Benigno Aquino, speaker of the Philippine Assembly, he was a lawyer in civilian life. He had a fast, flexible intellect, lots of drive, a likeable personality, and a remarkable sense of humor. Before Catalan and I left for the new CP, I went over the situation with him and with Malinit. The movement had been well planned and should have been executed with minimum confusion.

But when we reached the rendezvous point—the bridge—we found no one. Not one lick of work had been done. Before we had found the officers and guides, the battery arrived and halted on the bridge. Aquino and Malinit arrived breathlessly to report that cutting the trail through the woods would have taken much work, but there was a ford across the river leading directly to the position. I had found the ford and rejected it earlier, but now it had to be used. Each vehicle had to cross a hundred yards of heavy sand on each side, negotiate a fast current, and enter deep woods, all in pitch blackness. Vehicles got stuck in the sand and had to be pushed or towed. Finally, our Dodge truck had to tow them across one at a time. It was by long odds the poorest of many poor movements. I lost my temper and promised Aquino a punch in the nose as soon as we were straightened out. He answered, "Sir, I wish you would. I deserve it." The answer cooled me down.

I still cannot understand Aquino's actions that night. After the Japanese occupation of Manila, his father took a post in Vargas's cabinet. After the surrender, the first thing I saw when I entered the prisoner of war stockade at San Fernando was

Lieutenant Aquino, wearing a white suit with a Japanese arm band. He told me that because he spoke Japanese he had been placed in charge of the prisoners' mess. I had not known he spoke Japanese, and I did not know how, in the space of twenty-four or thirty-six hours, the Japanese had discovered Aquino, out of the confused mass of 70,000 soldiers and 20,000 civilians, and placed him in a position of responsibility.

Later, in prison camp, Colonel O'Day told me that Aquino had been suspected of being a Japanese agent, that instructions had been received from USAFFE G-2 to watch him closely, and that these instructions had been passed on to Catalan. Catalan never told me of this, nor did he relieve Aquino of a staff assignment that permitted him to roam at will, night and day, in his own car and with his own servant, anywhere on Bataan. If Aquino was a traitor, he completely fooled me.*

By the next morning, we had established communications, but we couldn't get through to Hughes. Investigation disclosed that he had moved without notifying us. We eventually found him about two kilometers west of the beach on the Damalog trail. He seemed content to have the artillery decentralized under local beach commanders. Of necessity, I adopted the same policy and devoted my energies to encouraging local infantry commanders to coordinate defense with the artillery.

This was our unhappiest CP. Heavy brush and timber restricted the view of the sky; though we could hear planes almost constantly, we couldn't see them. We became less and less alert. On the afternoon of January 18 we paid the penalty. The scream of diving bombers was our first warning. I saw Datoon, my orderly, dive past me for a trench, absolutely horizontally and at least three feet off the ground. By the time I hit the trench, he was in the bottom, digging with his fingers.

---

*Antonio Aquino was far from being a traitor; during the Bataan campaign he performed some heroic feats that were, of course, unknown to the author at that time. After surviving the Death March, he was singled out by the Japanese on the basis of his father's nominal collaboration, but refused to cooperate except in attempts to ameliorate conditions for the prisoners.—Ed.

I remember pulling him to a vertical position, patting him on the back, and saying, "It is all right now, son, it's all over." But my feeling belied my words.

Others were not all right. The radio sergeant had been killed instantly and one man so seriously wounded that he died en route to the hospital. One of our Scout NCO assistant instructors was wounded seriously enough to require hospitalization. Several others had minor injuries. I believed the man who died would have been saved if he could have been evacuated to a hospital promptly. We had no ambulance and had to unload a vehicle to take him to Limay.

Examinations of the bomb fragments from this attack showed the bombs seemingly made of little more than iron pipe filled with scrap iron and high explosive. I picked up one piece which was obviously from the hold-down straps of a Ford battery. Several other pieces were from farm machinery. I remembered the many shiploads of metal junk American businessmen had sold to Japan in recent years and hoped that they would choke on their steak and potatoes.

We moved that night to a position on the Damalog trail near Hughes's CP. The situation on the front line was serious. The Japanese were pressing vigorously each day, slowly but surely extending westward. There were daily reports of some portion of our front being dented, requiring counterattacks to restore the line—counterattacks which were not always completely successful. Because we lacked a general reserve, each attack and counterattack depleted local reserves and thus the ability to keep our long line intact. Finally we heard of a breakthrough on the front of Mt. Natib, at the junction of the 41st and 51st Divisions. The gap was closed, but several hundred Japanese sifted down the valley of the Abo-Abo River. They scattered and operated as snipers, causing considerable annoyance but not much damage.

I visited II Corps' CP in an attempt to improve beach defense coordination, going over my problems with Colonel Daugherty, the corps artillery officer, and Johnny Ball, his assistant. Daugherty was eager to assist but was primarily occupied with conditions at the front. Word had just been received that the Abo-Abo penetration endangered the entire line. I saw the G-3 situation map and the latest information posted. Viewing it purely and simply as a Leavenworth map problem, the situation was ripe for a general counterattack across the base of the penetration. The terrain was favorable, and there was a mass of artillery, with excellent observation points, to prepare the way. The only thing lacking was the force to counterattack.

As long as the hacienda–Mt. Natib line held, the artillery could operate to fine effect. As soon as we were forced to withdraw to the Mt. Samat position, we would be hamstrung. I tried to reconnoiter up to the head of the Damalog trail and found an impenetrable jungle. Pack artillery might get partway in, but not vehicles.

On the morning of January 23 I visited the corps' CP and found Colonel Daugherty. He indicated on his map the line to which the army would retire. The hinge and dominating feature of this line was Mt. Samat. I had been over this line several times. It had a fine field of fire for infantry from the bay until the junction of the back road near the front slope of Mt. Samat. From there west the jungle closed in, and practically no field of fire remained at all. West of Mt. Samat, the Pantingan River, with heavy close sides and a broad open valley, provided a made-to-order corridor for the Japanese to attack.

Daugherty said our regiment would revert to the 21st Division upon withdrawal, and he showed me the area on the southeast slope of Mt. Samat where we would go. After one glance at the map, I told him it would take several weeks to cut our way in. In reply, he dug out a reconnaissance report detailing a trail into the area, with descriptions and coordinates for about twenty gun positions. Red-faced, I copied the information and phoned the regimental reconnaissance officer and the battalion commanders to meet me for a look at the area.

We found the trail quickly and started south. After about a hundred yards the trail turned into a faint footpath. Following it for about a kilometer, we realized we couldn't get vehicles over it without engineer assistance and about three weeks' time.

When I returned to Daugherty and reported this, we re-examined his reconnaissance report. A closer look at its map revealed the report had been drawn up for mule artillery and the positions were for pack howitzers. We concluded that the best that could be done was to occupy a position near San Vincente, ask for engineer assistance, and each day push into the jungle as far as possible. General Parker came in and drew Daugherty outside; when the colonel returned, he had an overlay map showing the new positions and a notation that the withdrawal would start at 7 P.M. the next day, January 24.

Preliminaries for occupation of these positions had no sooner begun, however, than our orders were changed again. Now we were to be back on beach defense, overlapping the 2nd Regular Division extending to the north and a battalion of the 31st Infantry (American) covering the gap between Pandan and Limay.

I sent officers scurrying for the battalion commanders. It was past noon, and time would not permit me to wait for them and then make a reconnaissance of almost nine thousand yards of beach. I refreshed my memory of the general setup by a wild dash—hindered considerably by Herman—along the beach road and then divided the total area into battalion sectors, leaving to the battalion commanders the detailed reconnaissance and selection of positions.

That night we were told to contact Lieutenant Colonel Doane, executive of the 31st Infantry (American), at a CP near ours. From him we learned the orders for that regiment had been changed: it was to be withdrawn into corps reserve, and the beach defense from Pandan to Limay would be taken over by the 31st Infantry (Philippine). The commanding officer of that regiment, Col. Jack Irwin, wanted to see us.

We found him the next morning as he was walking his front line. Things looked pretty bad. His men were exhausted and he himself was almost out on his feet. He gave us his dispositions:

two battalions on the front line sandwiching a composite group of Philippine Army Air Corps ground troops organized as infantry. The 2nd Battalion, commanded by Major McKee, was on beach defense. For reserve he had nothing.

His responsibility for beach defense went only to Limay; ours, to the Alangan River. He asked us to work out the artillery coordination on the beach with McKee. We went over the general plan of front-line support—our secondary mission—and left the details until after we arranged the beach defense with McKee.

I was depressed by the condition of the front-line defense. The infantrymen were almost done in physically. An attack pressed with vigor would have met little resistance. But for some reason, the Japanese in front of that sector did not follow from the hacienda line for some days, and then only with patrol feelers.

McKee had only one battalion to cover three thousand yards of beach. The East road was the only supply route to the front line and, in most places, was within two or three hundred yards of the beach. A night landing, a quick push inland, and our supply route would be cut.

Until this time I had been concerned but not really worried about beach defense. I could not see where the Japanese would get sufficient water transportation to do more than put a raid ashore from Manila Bay, for I had been told that all the harbor boats, tugs, and interisland ships in the bay had been sunk or taken to Corregidor when Manila was evacuated.

I was astonished, therefore, when our observation posts reported several large vessels moving from Manila toward Guagua. Through my glasses they looked oceangoing, and I could see they mounted guns of fieldpiece size.

As the days passed, twelve vessels of interisland size, plus many tugs, barges, and other boats were seen on Manila Bay. The larger vessels had been converted into gunboats—we called them the wooden battleships—that harassed the Bataan coast every few nights. The tugs and barges plied daily between Manila, Guagua, and Orani, just outside our range. Thus, the Japanese held a constant threat against our vulnerable flank and supply road. They feinted attacks against our flank repeatedly, fired from the wooden battleships every few nights, made several minor landing attempts—on three occasions, major efforts.

The failure to destroy the water transportation in Manila resulted in immobilizing on beach defense one Philippine army division (the 2nd Regular), a battalion of the 31st Infantry (Philippine), thirty-nine pieces of artillery full time and eighteen additional pieces part time, as well as three searchlights, and a large number of tanks. Seizure of the enemy ships would have released the bulk of these troops to the front line where they were badly needed.

Initially, our artillery responsibility went only as far as the Alangan River. It was based upon the presumption that the Corregidor guns, which could reach as far north as Limay, could give support below that point. It was immediately evident that the coordination of the Corregidor guns and our own with the infantry at the beaches presented a big problem. Our only line of communication was a single bare-wire line on poles along the East road, controlled by the army and operated by the Signal Corps. To speak from my CP to the Corregidor fire control station, I had to go through five switchboards. Another thing that slowed telephone service throughout the campaign was the innate politeness of the Filipino. It was very rude to conclude an official call without inquiring into the health of the other party, discussing the situation, and relaying the latest rumors.

As Japanese air activity intensified, most of the harassing bombings occurred along the East road, and almost every bomb took out a section of the telephone wire. The Signal Corps did yeoman service in keeping the line repaired, but every time it went out communication stopped. As a result, I did not have one satisfactory telephone communication to Corregidor during the entire campaign.

It became evident early that the Manila Bay artillery defense had stopped too far north. The Lamao docks, the Lamao River delta, the corps ration, the gasoline and ammunition dumps, and the entire corps headquarters and corps service units in the Lamao Valley were south of the limit of artillery protection. North of Limay we were able to work out an effective and closely coordinated system of observation and fire control. Great credit must be given to Bonner for the communication net he perfected, not only over our own wires, but over the wires of other units, by persuading them to tie into our system. Our first efforts were to connect three widely separated CPs into our own fire-direction center so that we could, through triangulation, quickly determine the approximate location of hostile vessels on the bay. Daily this system was improved.

As time went on, practice and continuous instruction improved the standard of our switchboard and telephone operators greatly. I must emphasize that this reasonably satisfactory communication system prevailed only from Limay north. South of Limay conditions were very unsatisfactory in the sector of the 2nd Regular Division, particularly in the Lamao subsector under command of Lieutenant Colonel Garcia. In justice to these units and their commanders, I must point out that these troops were organized after war started and were woefully short of technical equipment, especially telephones, switchboard, and wire. Nevertheless, I consider that these organizations failed to take energetic action to overcome obstacles to communication.

Bonner went over the beach carefully and submitted a plan which, by moving some of our own installations and loaning some equipment, we could coordinate with the infantry, even if not entirely satisfactorily. Catalan, Bonner, and I visited Garcia to discuss coordination and work out details of cooperation. We found Garcia completely satisfied with his defense measures, apathetic to any idea of coordination with the artillery, and entirely unaware of the weakness of his communication system.

As with communication, so it was with the actual defense installations. We were unable to the very end to accomplish coordination of artillery fire with the infantry because there was no organized plan of infantry fire. Each rifleman was his own army.

The efficiency of these Philippine units was low. Their officers were militarily ignorant of this fact because they had no standards to shoot for. Complacently satisfied with existing conditions, to the very end they were never engaged against the enemy. Their attention was focused not upon military improvement but upon their political-military advancement. I heard more conversation about their promotions and chances of getting the same pay as American officers than I did about the location of machine guns.

These units caused me countless hours of anxiety, and I could not alter my opinion that, even at the end of the campaign, the defense south of Limay was incapable of offering effective resistance to an enemy landing. It was providence that the landing attempts were made north of Limay, where they were effectively met.

Approximately a week after the withdrawal to the Mt. Natib line, I was summoned to a conference with the corps commander, General Parker. Catalan and Bonner accompanied me. Also present were General Francisco, commanding the 2nd Regular Division; his sector commanders; Major Ganahl, commanding the SPM battalion; and the corps chief of staff and G-3. Parker conducted the conference personally, and it was the only time I knew him to show anger.

He opened the session by referring rather generally to a sheaf of inspection reports furnished by members of his staff after visits to the beach defense units. Without mentioning specific units, he commented on "reprehensible laxity." The items he mentioned corresponded exactly to my views. The general then stressed the importance of the beach defense and declared that failure to produce improvement would force him to turn the job over to officers who could. (In a private interview later, in which I asked for specific faults noted in the artillery, Parker assured me his remarks were not directed at the artillery, that he was thoroughly satisfied with our efforts, and that we were the one "bright spot in a damned black cloud.")

Details of beach defense were then discussed. The artillery protection of the south beach area was a matter of Parker's concern. The fact that the Lamao River docks and valley were a logical objective was obvious, as was the fact that artillery fire from Corregidor could not be depended upon. It was equally obvious that if we pulled our guns farther south, we would be stretching them pretty thin. After some discussion, Parker asked me for a recommendation.

I could envision a successful beach defense only under a system of unified command of infantry, tanks, SPMs, and artillery. Such a system required adequate communications and the ability to function instantly without recourse to higher command—a system whereby troops could be moved quickly to limit hostile penetration after a landing and then attack across the base of the penetration, at the same time concentrating artillery fire from the flanks against the penetration, especially across its base to prevent reinforcement.

Therefore I recommended—

1. that the artillery be stretched southward to Cabcaben;

2. that a provisional battalion be formed from other artillery units available. There were four naval guns on demountable wheels, and a battery of 2.95-inch howitzers of the 2nd Field Artillery Combat Team of the Philippine 2nd Regular Division. (The latter was composed largely of ROTC boys, who had volunteered after the schools were closed, and was known as the ROTC Battery. It was noted for its spirit and morale and ended the war with a fine record);

3. that the provisional battalion be incorporated into the 21st Field Artillery;
4. that available naval guns on pedestal mounts be secured and placed at critical beach locations. There were five of these: three 3-inch, 21-caliber pieces and two 3-inch, 50-caliber submarine deck guns, all with a 360-degree traverse;
5. that the SPM battalion be held in reserve for roving assignments.

After a good deal of discussion, these recommendations were accepted and ordered into effect by General Parker. Despite my urging, however, the beach defense units were never placed under a unified command. While I was empowered with general supervision of all artillery, I had no command status until late in March and could only suggest, recommend, and report. I never did know who commanded the beach defense tanks in my area, or whom to call upon had they been needed. The entire system was based on cooperation instead of command. This was in contrast to the west coast of Bataan, where a unified command succeeded in expelling several tenaciously held enemy landings.

February and March were relatively uneventful on the front line. Our immediate front, the East road tidewater, was quiet. I concluded that the enemy had suffered fairly heavily in the attacks on the hacienda line, since our withdrawal of January 24 was followed very slowly. In the tidewater, called Subsector A, the Japanese did not even push patrols up to our main line, but were content to occupy Balanga and work patrols up to Pilar. In the center, where the heavy, close country gave fine cover, they were more active. Vigorous patrolling and small local attacks felt out our line. The outpost line was driven in many times in various places but restored by local counterattacks. Many spirited actions, seldom larger than regimental or sector size, resulted and were excellent combat training, building up a "veteran" spirit among the troops.

The mass weight of the enemy was obviously located in our center, facing the junction of the two corps. We heard of vigorous action in the west against I Corps. One penetration there was not vigorously followed up, enabling us to close the gap, surround the penetrating force, and reduce it. We also heard of landings on the China Sea coast, principally at Agaloma Bay, where fine artillery action prevented the enemy from being reinforced, and where foot-by-foot jungle fighting finally reduced the penetrations.

Finally, a sizable attack developed in front and west of Mt. Samat. This was repulsed with ease and was regarded as local in character until the G-2 people, from captured maps and copies of the attack order, determined it was a major effort—a coordinated all-out attack—to crack the Mt. Samat line with the forces available. When it failed the enemy broke off contact, except in the west, and pulled back completely from our front. We pushed our patrols forward and found the Japanese had established a strong outpost line on the south slopes of Mt. Natib and then refused northeastward toward Orani.

On one of my trips to the rear during this period, I jokingly asked Col. Frank Brezina, the Luzon Force quartermaster, when the relief expedition was due. He laughed the question off, but shortly afterward mentioned that he was moving the quartermaster installations farther southeast, to high ground, in anticipation of the rainy season. The six-month siege period required by the war plan would end early in June, and the rains would normally be on us in July and August. The inference was obvious. The prospect of relief was a mirage.

Subsequently, we learned of the change in war policy, accepted by the United States in view of the British and Dutch participation in the war, of the loss of Singapore and the Dutch East Indies, and of the inclusion of the American-Philippine Force in the Allied Southwest Pacific command of General Wavell. The policy had but one objective: the defense of Australia. We in the Philippines were left to do the best we could. The best could only be to hold out as long as possible in the forlorn hope that something would throw a cog into the enemy machine and start it unexpectedly in reverse. Holding out meant the maximum conservation of effort, and that could not permit offensive action with its wastage of personnel and material.

Food was an all-important factor. One day in March I bluntly asked Brezina how many days' ration we had left. In confidence, he told me that it was less than fourteen, that we were already drawing upon Corregidor reserve stocks, and that, unless supply ships got through from Cebu, we faced disaster because enemy bombing made it difficult to keep the supply line open. One or two ships from Cebu had made it through the enemy blockade, and there was a story that the navy was converting six submarines into supply ships. As it turned out, the blockade tightened, and supply by submarine on a regular schedule never materialized. There was another factor of vital importance to us artillerymen. During a visit to corps CP, I was shown a copy of a high command directive seriously curtailing expenditure of artillery ammunition. The letter showed the amounts of each caliber on hand and the percentage expended. Even for a six-month siege, our expenditure schedule looked like a second lieutenant's bank balance—badly overdrawn. We had been firing at everything that stuck up its head —patrols, machine guns, truck columns—to fulfill our role as infantry support. By doing so, we had maintained artillery superiority. But now we had to limit our fire to what was vital to an infantry mission. Counterbattery fire decreased because we had to locate the hostile battery accurately now instead of throwing a lot of metal into an area of several hundred square yards. Infantry calls for fire on minor targets had to be refused. The results were bad since the infantry did not have its own heavy weapons—mortars, antitank guns—to handle the support we had been providing. Consequently, the Japanese became more active and so did their infantry. And in the big picture, the shortage of artillery ammunition alone precluded an offensive.

Another factor that weighed heavily was the gasoline short-age. As the gasoline allowance decreased each week, the beach defense situation deteriorated. It was the practice of the tanks and SPMs to stay under cover during daylight and to move to beach positions at dusk. Similarly, I moved my guns frequent-ly, making lavish use of alternate and dummy positions. This movement was essential. Planes were over us constantly, and when even a battery fired, they swooped down like vultures. Sometimes the battery received a few bombs "right now," but it was more normal to expect artillery fire within a few hours and heavy bombing the next dawn. Constant shifting of posi-tions was our only way to keep our guns alive. I did not allow kitchens or individual cooking at gun positions. Cooking was done well to the rear, where the smoke would not betray a combat position. Food for the men at the guns and rations from the service command dumps had to be brought up by truck. There were no animals.

But as our regimental gasoline allowance dropped to fifty gallons a week, then to thirty, each battalion had to stop all tactical movement and use gas only for ammunition supply, moving the kitchens to the combat positions. My inspection visits dropped to one weekly trip along the entire defense area instead of a detailed inspection of each unit weekly. Our guns, the tanks, and the SPMs remained in combat positions, where smoke from the cooking fires became invitations to bombing. Losses mounted, efficiency decreased, morale dropped away. If there was ever a period when my regiment needed firm guid-ance and ever-present leadership, this was it—but the situation made it impossible for commanders to maintain this vital con-tact with their personnel.

During the lull in activities, while the Japanese were gather-ing their strength, we used the time in my regiment to do what the outbreak of war had prevented: train our officers and men. There was little chance of an enemy surprise from the bay dur-ing daylight. Consequently, we rested the men as much as we could in daylight hours and tried to do the same thing for the officers. We were very short of officers, however, because of the additional batteries we had absorbed. It was often a problem to maintain officer observation posts, have an executive at each battery, perform administrative duties, and still let the officers get some rest. Despite all this, I was hardhearted enough to require a two-hour officer's school in each battalion, with the emphasis on gunnery. All enlisted men were trained as cannoneers regardless of their normal assignments. Some men were also trained as spares in the communication details. We finally developed two well-trained gun crews in each battery and one relief crew, which usually was used—when its services were not required elsewhere—as the "alert" crew during daylight hours. Most of the training took place at night. One gun crew had the trick from 6 P.M. to midnight; the second, from midnight to 6 A.M. During daylight one sentinel per gun remained on duty, with an alert crew resting in the vicinity. The crews alternated on the night tricks.

From January 26 to March 22, we had a fine CP on Trail 10. The hill dropped off very sharply from the trail which ran along the northwestern crest of the valley, and gave us excellent defilade. Several hundred yards from the bottom of the trail was a fine bathing pool. We enjoyed daily cold plunges there for a while until Herman discovered us. After that we had to outguess him, and our bathing became less regular. It was the climb back up the hill from the pool that finally made me realize how weak I was getting. I knew that I had been forced to take a sizable tuck in my waistband, and that my daily visits to the battalions were tiring me, but when I had to stop and rest before negotiating the hill after bathing, it was apparent that our starvation ration had sapped my strength.

Joe Tacey dropped in on us one day and told us he was putting a 155-mm. battery 200 yards east of us and another about 300 yards to our west. We started looking for a new CP. The area in which the 155s were located invariably became very unhealthy—steel poisoning usually developed quickly. Tacey told me the limitation on ammunition permitted hostile artillery far greater activity, and the enemy was quick to take advantage of the restrictions on our counterbattery fire. The enemy 105 rifles became particularly active. This gun, which far outranged our antiquated 155s, was most effective. It had a very high muzzle velocity and, even at long ranges, the terminal velocity did not drop much below the speed of sound, so you barely heard the shell coming before it was in your lap.

For a while, we sat tight in our CP after the 155s moved in, but very soon Herman and his bombing companions started combing the area for them. The aerial observers also began lifting up the tree branches and looking underneath for the guns. A lot of steel was sprayed around our swimming pool, putting fragments through our kitchen and killing a number of civilian refugees, including a woman and child. Then the enemy 105s opened up. I was absent from the CP the first time it was shelled. There were no casualties, but the personnel were visibly shaken. The next afternoon the 105s opened up again. This time several men were slightly wounded. Three men were buried alive when a shell hit seven feet from their V trench. They were dug out, resuscitated, and remained on duty. After that the bombers worked over our kitchen area again.

We decided to move. I was reluctant, for our communications were functioning so well I was loath to disturb them. However, I was glad I agreed when later in the afternoon the bombers laid a load of white phosporous along the hillside across the river and above our swimming pool, setting fire to the dry underbrush. This caused no casualties, but it burned the insulation off all the telephone wire in the area.

It was during this period of about ten days, while we sat and took the shelling and bombing, that I learned to admire Bonner's nerveless courage. Bombers are not bad unless they are diving for your "spot." You can watch their line of flight and either be an interested spectator of their technique—if they are not lined up on you—or take to your hole and brace yourself. But with shelling—especially from the fast 105s— you can't see the line of flight. You can only hear the express-train rush of the approaching shell, and that for only a second or two before the impact. My instinct—and I am not ashamed of it, I taught it to my men—was to hit the trench or the ground at the first whine of a nearing shell, and then figure out later whether it was necessary. No so Bonner. He had no nerves, and he had an uncanny sense of direction of the approaching shell. I hit the dirt many times for shells at least a hundred yards away, but Bonner seldom moved unless the line of flight lined up very close to us. I finally acquired a little better sense of direction and, by watching Bonner, saved myself many brushoffs. He failed me once though, and as we picked ourselves up, with the smoke and dirt still settling around us, I decided to follow my own reactions in the future. But I continued to admire Bonner's phlegmatic calm under fire.

Our new CP at a position called KP 150 was, in one respect, just what I had been searching for throughout the campaign. It was on a hill that sloped two ways, eastward toward the bay and southwest toward the valley in which Garcia's CP was located. From the crest I had a fine view of the bay, from well to the west of the Mt. Arayat line, extending to Manila, Cavite, and almost to Cabcaben. Thus, with the exception of a small sector to the south, the entire area of our assigned beach defense was under my eye. This was of especial advantage as time went on and the gasoline shortage limited my movements.

In the afternoon sun we had a beautiful view of Manila. The reflection upon the tall buildings made them a glorious dazzling white. In our half-starved condition these shining white buildings seemed like Valhalla—the Holy Grail of our efforts and sacrifices.

Before we came back to this CP, and while we were on Trail 10, the beginning of the end was apparent. I do not mean that we became conscious of defeat, or gave up. Far from it—we continued to hope and have faith in our leaders, in our ability to hold out, and in our government's efforts to send a relief expedition that would arrive in storybook fashion. But, despite this faith and hope, we were intelligent, trained officers, capable of estimating the military situation and arriving at a logical conclusion. We knew the only possible eventual effects of our acute food shortage and dwindling stores of ammunition and gasoline. We knew combat strength was deteriorating each day as starvation, dysentery, and malaria took their toll. But while we knew that time was working quickly against us, we hoped it was working equally quickly for us; in our estimate of the situation, there was but one favorable fact: sooner or later the relief expedition would have to arrive.

We listened to the San Francisco radio and were told that the crippling raid on Pearl Harbor was not crippling. We listened to an eye-witness account of the arrival of what we believed to be the relief armada in Australian waters, an account telling of ships "as far as the eye could see." We listened to the hooey put out by our own radio, the Voice of Freedom—propaganda so thick that it served no purpose except to disgust us and incite mistrust. We listened to the Japanese propaganda radio in Manila, beamed to us in English. Its theme song was "I'm Waiting for Ships that Never Come In." We watched with growing concern the Japanese advance to the south. We shook off the sinking of the *Prince of Wales* and the *Repulse* early in the war as an unlucky break. We could not with reason expect Hong Kong to hold out long, but its Christmas Day surrender was even sooner than we anticipated.

But we still counted with smug satisfaction upon the assistance of our allies. Instead of having the long ocean hop from Honolulu, facing the Japanese navy on the way, our expedition could come via Australia, the Dutch East Indies, and Singapore. We all knew the strength of Singapore, the key point of the British Empire in the Far East.

Further, we had a comfortable feeling about the strength of the Dutch army and navy. We believed that the Dutch army, although small, was thoroughly modern, organized and equipped on European lines, and strong in automatic firepower. Its air service especially was supposed to be a tower of strength, with fields from which our own planes could cover the movement north of the relief expedition.

Thus, as the news from the south trickled in, we found it almost unbelievable. We plotted the positions of the English forces in the Malayan jungle and persuaded ourselves that their twenty-to-thirty-mile-per-day retirement was simply outpost action, serving to delay the enemy; that when the defense lines around Singapore were reached, all the foolishness would stop. Singapore would hold. Our expedition would gather in Australia. Under naval protection, covered by land-based aircraft, the expedition would come northward to our relief.

And then on February 15 Singapore fell. A stunned silence greeted the radio announcement. It could not be possible, but it was. The chain of our relief line was broken.

The Japanese tidal wave continued. From our beleaguered peninsula it looked as if the Dutch resistance was little better than a token action. The enemy took over Java, Sumatra, and Borneo, entered Timor on February 22, and was poised for the attack upon Australia. Our estimate of the situation had to be materially revised. Our relief expedition could not steam in now under air and naval protection; it would have to fight every step of the way. Instead of Australia being used as an expedition base, it was now a place to be defended.

But we still kept our tails up. I still had unfaltering faith in the leadership of MacArthur, despite the widespread criticism of his staff, and the political entanglements which many times seemed to warp his military judgment. I had worked so close to him for two years that I had implicit confidence in his ability, and unwavering faith that he would reach down and pull the rabbit out of the hat.

To the Filipino—officer and man—MacArthur was a legend. His father had established America in the Philippines. He himself had served many years there in junior and senior grades, up to that of department commander. To the great disappointment of Quezon, he had declined the post of governor general.

He had been selected by the Filipinos as their military adviser, the father of the army of which they were so proud. His personality was a source of inspiration to them. They were as dominated by his magnetism as I was, even more so, if that were possible. He was the fountainhead of their organization and the driving force behind their will to fight. It is almost impossible to convey the reverence in which he was held or the adulation he inspired.

About March 12 we began to hear rumors that MacArthur was leaving. On the 13th Bonner was at Corregidor, the first time any of my officers had gone there. When he returned, he called me to one side and told me of overhearing MacArthur saying good-by to an officer and of MacArthur's orderly drawing a set of web field equipment for the general. On the 14th the grapevine told us—faster than a field order could have been disseminated—the news that the commander in chief, Mrs. MacArthur, their young son, Quezon, and a military and political staff were en route to Australia.

A few days later, when he had arrived safely, we were officially told of the exodus. The propaganda radio did a good job. It built up the president's order giving MacArthur command of the allied forces, stressed the advantage of having him in command of the relief expedition, emphasized his request to the president to be allowed to remain with his beloved Filipino-Americans, reiterated the president's insistence that MacArthur assume the command in Australia, and then went into a eulogy about the trained soldier carrying out his superior's orders regardless of where his heart lay. They gave us his famous "I go, but I shall return" utterance.

But despite the buildup, despite our explanation to the Filipino officers and men of the more important command and of the value of having their military god at the controls of the machine that would relieve us, despite everything, it was sad news, and the Filipino reaction was as expected. Not outwardly. They gave lip service—but the heart went out of them.

We continued our efforts; the lines still held. Cebu and the airfields in Mandanao were still in our hands. Shortly after MacArthur's arrival in Australia, the grapevine told us that a radio report had been received from him to the effect that the food reserve period could be reduced one month with safety— from June 1 to July 1. Morale increased. We could stand on our heads until June 1.

Then came the final and deciding morale blow of the campaign. Every radio on Bataan was tuned to President Roosevelt's fireside speech on the status of the war, every ear within range alert to catch the message. When it came, it was the death knell of Bataan. He placed a large and emphatic period for all to see at the end of the handwriting on the wall. He invited his listeners to follow him upon their maps of the world. He outlined the magnitude of the American task. He spoke of American groups in Greenland, Ireland, England; of help to Russia, to China, to India. He spoke of the trackless miles of ocean between America and Japan, of the almost insurmountable difficulty of relieving the Philippines, of the vital necessity of defending Australia. And he gave his own and America's undying promise that ultimately the Philippines would be redeemed.

Anything he said after that was anticlimactic, as we knew that from then on our action would be the epilogue. The curtain had rung down and it was only a matter of time. There was no prospect of relief within the time limit human endurance would permit. Yet, until within twelve hours of the actual act of surrender, I did not hear an officer or man on Bataan utter the word "surrender" or discuss the possibilities.

In prison camp, after many discussions, I know most officers and men reasoned the thing out something like this: one alternative was to fight it out to annihilation; the other was to hold out as long as possible and then surrender. If there was any military justification for annihilation, we were ready for the sacrifice. If not, then we could hope only for quick release after capture. For the Filipinos, surrender was the much brighter prospect. At the pleasure of Japan, they could expect to be released and returned to their homes. For the 14,000 Americans on Bataan and Corregidor it didn't make much difference. To many, which would be preferable, death or capture, was a toss-up. Which it was to be was not our decision but that of our leaders, and I think most Americans did as I did—shrugged it off and waited for General King and General Wainwright to make the choice.

Among the Americans there developed an ironic what-the-hell attitude. It was all taken as a grim jest—on us. We knew the worst and laughed at each other as we faced it. There was no bitterness. The only chagrin I ever saw displayed was always on the same subject—indignation that our enemy and the unknowing world would see in our collapse a defeat for American arms, that our own people, in ignorance of actual conditions, would see a failure of regular army troops and regular army officers.

Actually, I was never prouder of being an American than when I was one of that small group who, with a jest on their lips, awaited the inevitable. In those days were born the Battling Bastards of Bataan, whose little ditty tells their story:

> Here's to the Battling Bastards of Bataan:
> No momma, no poppa, no Uncle Sam,
> No aunts, no uncles, no cousins, no nieces,
> . . . and nobody gives a damn.*

Now, after MacArthur's departure and the president's speech, came the hardest work of the war. The American instructors made more strenuous efforts during this time than during any other period of the campaign. We had to hold up Philippine morale, hold the units together. The final Japanese attack preparation could not be far off. Our G-2 service told

---

*This verse was written by an American correspondent, Frank Hewlett. The author has omitted the penultimate line: "No rifles, no guns, or artillery pieces."—Ed.

us of Japanese shock troops, which had reduced Singapore, arriving on Luzon. Day by day the artillery at our front increased. Enemy truck columns shuttled back and forth continuously, building up supplies and ammunition for a major effort.

But the rains were almost upon us. If we could beat off one more big attack, it might be the last one that could be launched until after the rainy season. By then things could happen. Work. Hold on just a little longer. Tighten your belts. The submarines will start getting food and supplies in. The air service will get here soon.

So we worked. A pat on the back, a cheery word here, an admonition there.

It was futile—the heart was gone, the will to do had ceased to exist. The Filipino command, high and low, began to concern itself with matters extraneous to the battlefield. Political differences, food, a decoration here and none there, promotion problems, differences in pay between American and Filipino officers, criticism of tactical decisions by the American high command, fault with the conduct of individual American officers—these things, not the state of defense, became our paramount problems.

That brings me to the almost overnight change in my relations with Colonel Catalan. It was but a small incident in the big story of the campaign, but it was an incident indicative of the condition of the army—a condition as much a factor as starvation, sickness, and depletion of resources in its contribution to the eventual collapse.

During the days at the beach on Manila Bay, during the bitter fighting of the withdrawal, and through the early days on Bataan, Catalan was most responsive to my advice—and yes, commands. He was not only responsive, but eager and willing. But during the quiet days on the Bataan beach defense this attitude changed.

Had I failed him, there would have been an obvious reason

for this. But I had not. The regiment had performed every mission more than creditably. By no conceivable fancy can it be charged that I let him down; quite the contrary. At a conference at corps CP early in March, when Colonel Daugherty was pressing for Catalan's relief, the general said he could not relieve Catalan without cause, that the regiment had a splendid record, that neither it nor Catalan had ever failed. Daugherty's answer was, "Hell no, and for a damned good reason. Mallonée has never let him fail."

The truth of this is indicated by the fact that when the line broke and the situation became chaotic in the last few days before the capitulation, the command again became mine. The baby was handed right back to me as soon as the diaper was soiled. Again, there was no objection to my giving commands —objection, hell, there was nothing but eagerness to obey.

I placed some of the responsibility for Catalan's change in attitude upon Villa-Real and the remainder upon the officers of the 2nd Regular Division. This division was a beehive of Filipino military politics, from the top down. Resentful of American leadership and domination, its officers, untried by battle, resorted to passive obstruction—cutting off their noses to spite their faces. They bragged openly that they had "gotten rid" of an American instructor whose sole defense, by their own story, was that he tried to get results from the training program.

I was made aware of my change in status in many small ways. Orders and tactical information arriving at the CP, unless they were specifically marked for me, were filed without my having been given a chance to see them. The daily G-2 summary and information sheet was shown to Catalan but not to me, until I raised so much hell, he instructed the staff to get my initials before it was filed. Even then it would be long delayed and almost invariably I would have to send for it.

This sidetracking of orders caused Bonner to miss a promotion, for a letter which should have resulted in my initiating a request for his promotion to lieutenant colonel was suppressed,

I believe deliberately, out of jealousy because Villa-Real, who corresponded in assignment to Bonner, had been promoted only to major. Savoie again forgot himself and slapped a man. Catalan wrote me a letter stating that he had decided to ask for Savoie's relief. I investigated and found, as I had expected, that Savoie had resorted to a flagrant violation of orders and duty. I discovered, too, that Captain Acosta, the Filipino battalion commander, also had often resorted to slapping and cursing. My recommendation was that Savoie be officially reprimanded, that Acosta be admonished, and that the incident be closed. These two youngsters made a fine team and had the best battalion in the regiment. To wreck that battalion on the eve of the battle upon which the fate of Bataan was to rest did not seem justified. I discussed this with Catalan and thought he concurred. However, Catalan sent a letter to corps, without my knowledge, asking for Savoie's relief.

Corps acted promptly and favorably upon the request, without giving Savoie a hearing or referring the matter to me. In my opinion the corps action smelled a little, for the Scout Artillery jumped at the chance of getting Savoie, giving him command of a battery—a rather peculiar action to take in the case of an officer supposed to be under a cloud.*

I was extremely resentful and telephoned Colonel Daugherty, telling him I was en route to corps with a request that I be relieved from my assignment and sent to the bonepile for "reclassification."

*The slapping incident was, in the opinion of the Filipino officers, far more serious than the author realized. Catalan stated in 1971 that he had to transfer Savoie to save his life from the enraged men of his battalion. A slapping was considered a blood insult to be avenged. Villa-Real stated that the men were in such an ugly mood over the incident, there was a real danger one of them might have shot Savoie in the back at night "for the honor of his officer."—Ed.

But when I arrived, Daugherty patted me on the back, praised my work, and smoothed my feathers. He said he had discussed my relief with the corps command, as a reward for my work, but that there was a stumbling block over the selection of my successor. He counted off on his fingers the officers available, commented on why each would not be expected to maintain the regiment's standard, and asked me to reconsider. He revealed that Catalan's action in the matter had been viewed as evidence of his inability to command. His relief had been recommended and was being considered higher up; if I would hang on for a few days longer, I would be given command of the regiment.

Catalan was, in fact, relieved April 6, and I was placed in command. By that time the front line had collapsed, the army was disintegrating, and the end was only a matter of days. The chaos reduced Catalan to his earlier dependency, and he tied himself again to my leading string. I was in virtual command when the order for his relief reached me. With the end so close and my wishes being executed as if I had been in official command, I saw no reason to break his heart. I never informed him of the order or let him know he had been relieved.

During one of my inspection trips of potential gun positions on the south shore, I stopped at Luzon Force CP to pay my respects to General King, who had been given command of the Luzon Force (that is, the defense of Bataan) when General Wainwright went to Corregidor to take over the newly constituted U.S. Forces in the Philippines (USFIP), which replaced USAFFE when that command, in the person of MacArthur, went south. It was with mingled emotions that I made my call. General King had been entrusted with a command among the highest his country could grant a soldier. For that he could be congratulated. But he had been given command of an already lost cause. For that he deserved sympathy and condolence that could not be expressed. On his shoulders was placed the burden to decide, when the collapse finally came, on annihilation or surrender. When on April 9 he made that decision, it was the first major surrender of American arms since April 9 of 1865, when Robert E. Lee had to give up another lost cause. Upon my return from seeing King we were delayed near Lamao. Bombing had set fire to the corps' ammunition dump in Roderiquez Park and had blocked the road with a huge crater. Traffic was paralyzed for several hours. Bonner and I worked our command car to about six hundred yards from the fire and sat there under the lee of a bluff. Exploding 155s sent splinters over our heads even at that distance. Every time we tried to ease closer to the fire, renewed bursts would drive us back. But finally we reached the burning dump. We could not possibly get the command car through the road crater, but there was a lane through the fire which seemed passable if the car could ease through two ditches. Bonner went back and brought up the car.

Bumanlag, the driver, had a fixed expression on his face, like grim death was hanging onto his toe. He didn't slow down for me but hit the first ditch at about 25 miles per hour, went through the fire, jumped the second ditch, and hightailed up the road. I managed to grasp the windshield and swing up on the running board as he passed me.

Bumanlag demonstrated courage many times. Of necessity, Bonner, Catalan, and I had to go many places where it was not always healthy. Our jobs demanded that we take chances—and that meant Bumanlag had to take the same. He did, without a murmur, and was always ready to go again.

I can quote verbatim an entry in my diary that described the situation during the last week:

"Our men are weak and sick. They are actually weak to the point of staggering when they walk after any necessary burst of energy. Dysentery, malaria, and beriberi have combined to produce a weakened army. The 31st American and the Scouts have had severe losses which, of course, cannot be replaced. In the Philippine army, likewise, there is no adequate source of replacements. The shortages of equipment, which existed at the beginning of the war, have been aggravated by the ravages of the campaign. Clothing is worn, torn, and ragged. Personal equipment is supplemented by makeshifts. Men are cooking what little rice they can get in bamboo tubes. Many without mess gear are eating off bamboo slabs and leaves. Bamboo tubes substitute for canteens. *Nipa* leaves do service for hats. Bare feet are more common than shoes. Salmon cans have a multitude of uses.

"On April 1st I went to the Base Hospital for an antitetanus shot. I stepped on the scales and weighed 182—an estimated 178 stripped. I weighed about 198 when war broke.

"On Palm Sunday I attended a service conducted by Chaplain Sobrepena. It was a fine service, the sermon based upon the expression 'he lost himself in the crowd.' It gave me food for considerable thought and emphasized in my thought that our leadership must not lose itself in the crowd. Despite the evidence of impending disaster all about us, we must not permit any letdown in effort. Despite everything we must keep going."

That was Palm Sunday—about ten days before the surrender. Sobrepena helped me to "keep going" to the end. He was one of the best, not only a spiritual leader, but a modern educator with a firm understanding of the world's social problems. He was an inspiration to me many times and the outstanding Filipino of my acquaintance. It was his depressing duty to bury our dead, and he had been recommended for decoration for the calm courage he displayed during burial services given under heavy fire.

Late in March the Japanese reestablished contact with our front line. The enemy mass was in the center, aimed down the Pantangan River corridor, as we expected.

Hostile aircraft became very active, and their tactics changed radically. Before this time, flights of three or nine planes would come directly to their selected objective and dump their load, or would fly around until they selected an objective. Between flights we were free to move around, reestablish positions, repair damage, and go about our business. The new method was spot bombing. Planes came over in successive flights, so there were always from nine to thirty-six in the air. They would float around lazily at low altitude, free from any American aerial interference. Our few antiaircraft guns were in the rear areas protecting dumps, depots, and the unused airfields. Every few minutes one plane would drop down, lift up the tree branches, and lay one or two eggs. Every vehicle that tried to move, every wire-laying detail, active machine gun, artillery flash, infantry patrol, food-carrying detail, column of smoke from small fires, even individual moving in the open, was a target.

In an effort to locate our artillery observation posts and bring them into the open, the enemy used white phosphorus on Mt. Crion and Mt. Samat. Large patches of underbrush burned off with an effect I doubt the Japanese expected. The phosphorus burned off the insulation on the telephone wire and completely broke down our conduct of artillery fire. This wire could not be replaced, and there was no radio for substitute communication.

This loss of communication was one reason why, by the time of the final enemy attack, our artillery was of limited efficiency. Other reasons were: loss of guns and observation posts, shortage of ammunition, lack of transportation and gasoline to bring forward what ammunition there was, and physical exhaustion of personnel. (The battalion farthest into the jungle had to have every round of ammunition carried to it for five to ten kilometers on the shoulders of men so weak they could barely walk.)

There were no accurate aerial photo mosaics, or even accurate maps; nor was there any equipment coming to the Philippines to make either. This complete absence of accurate mosaics and maps, after forty years of opportunity to create them, was something no engineer or air corps officer could ever explain to me. But even if we had possessed the most accurate maps or mosaics, we lacked the observation planes to locate and give the coordinates of targets.

A final vital factor was that the mass of our artillery could not range far enough to place its fire in the area from which we knew the Japanese attack would come.

The attack, when it did come, was preceded by the heaviest artillery bombardment I had heard about since the First World War. Our observers located thirty-eight batteries—75s and 105s, in positions designed for direct support of the infantry. These batteries were close up. Those in the rear—155s and 240s—could not be located except by aircraft, which we did not have. The artillery bombardment of the Pantangan River corridor was confined to an area about fifteen hundred yards wide, and was coupled with intensified aerial attack using large bombs, antipersonnel fragmentation bombs, and incendiary white phosphorous. The combination made this area a living hell, and when the infantry attack came, the line gave way quickly because there was only a shadow of a line left.

Some American staff and supply service officers criticized the Filipino troops who gave way as lacking the will to fight. That criticism was not heard from front-line officers. Although better-trained, better-equipped, stouter-hearted troops might have sustained the attack, I saw enough of the action in those fateful early days of April to know that the most seasoned troops would have been severely tried by the fury of that artillery and aerial preparation. On that vital fifteen hundred yards of front, hostile artillery laid a greater number of rounds per yard than we did at either St. Mihiel or the Argonne in 1918.

Later, some troops gave way with little or no justification, but whether the line across the corridor could have been held is a moot question. The facts are the line did not hold, there were no local reserves or secondary line, and the heart of the Bataan defense was laid bare.

The Japanese worked quickly. Second-wave troops crossed our old line and turned sharply southeast, attacking our line on the east of the penetration from behind and parallel to it. A regiment commanded by Colonel Ito, with two battalions abreast and one in close support, struck across the slope of Mt.

Samat toward Manila Bay. Other troops drove the penetration wedge deeper, cutting between the 41st Infantry and the remainder of II Corps, forcing that regiment—or the remnants of it—into the area of I Corps.

The 31st American went into counterattack to restore the line. By the time it got into position to attack along the San Vincente, the situation was changing every second. As it moved forward elements on both sides were giving way. Both its flanks were open, and before its attack got well under way, it met a double envelopment. Its attack had to be converted into a retrograde movement hoping to save as much as possible.

From there on all is confusion. The picture is lightened only in spots by what is known of the action of some small units that retained cohesion. There is not now nor ever will be a clear picture of the events of April 5 to 8. The essential element of command—communication—was nonexistent. Commanders reverted to a method of communication used before the advent of telephone and radio—the dispatch of aides, staff officers, or messengers to obtain information, convey orders, and maintain liaison. The jungle fastness defeated this effort.

With artillery communication out, guns remained silent for lack of information while a myriad of targets presented themselves. Artillery that had been laboriously tugged and pushed and pulled over cart tracks as far west as possible did not have a ghost of a chance of getting out. Regimental histories would be full of accounts of guns blown up while enemy infantry were using bayonets in the gun positions. I was told of crews who rammed a fuzed shell down the muzzles of guns and then fired another one against it. I was told of gunners who fired this gun-bursting projectile with the hand lanyard—and of one or two who strangely lived to tell about it. The 41st, 31st, and 51st Regiments—those pushed farthest into the jungle—suffered worst. The Scout Artillery nearer the tidewater had a chance and got out.

Finally the hostile attack reached the southwest slope of

Mt. Samat and turned east toward the top of the Damalog trail and Trail 10, joining in direction those troops driving east across the front of Samat.

Our SPMs and tanks were sent westward on Trail 10 and the Damalog trail to form strong points upon which the infantry could rally. Both did fine work. Both were eventually sacrificed. Without organized infantry support to protect them from the flanks and rear, and in the middle of a jungle, the vehicles were too vulnerable. One by one I saw these units leave the beach road and go up the trails to the destruction they knew awaited them. None came back. The jests on their lips, their what-the-hell attitude, takes a place in history with the Marine sergeant who led his men forward at Belleau Woods with the exhortation, "Come on, you bastards, do you want to live forever?"

On the beach we had our own action to occupy us. From March 27 to April 2 there was activity on the water nightly. One or two, sometimes more, of the wooden battleships would move in toward shore, fire for a short time, and move back. We were amused by their gunnery—not a shot fell on shore, only a few coming closer to land than four thousand yards. Several times their fire was aimed at their own territory in front of our front line. Many of the gun blasts on the ships were not followed by shell explosions, indicating that either a number of their rounds were duds or they were firing blanks. Since these bombardments were not sustained or followed up, it seemed they were for nuisance value, and, by appearing to threaten the beach, were meant to tie down units there that might otherwise have been sent to reinforce the front line.

A landing attempt finally came on the night of April 4. That day I had received an order from General King creating an artillery groupment, to be called Groupment A of II Corps, and placing me in command of it. It consisted of the 21st

Field Artillery, a provisional battalion composed of the ROTC battery as Battery E and the four naval landing guns as Battery H, and the six fixed naval pedestal guns used for beach defense. The order stated I was to "supervise and coordinate the action of all other artillery employed on beach defense between Pandon Point and Mariveles." This "other artillery" consisted of Ganahl's SPM battalion and a platoon of 155-mm. guns.

Around midnight of the 4th, the officer on duty at the regimental CP noticed that the texture of the water, which was dazzling in the moonlight, seemed to be getting darker, and called me to take a look. I started calling the north observation posts and met Harrison's incoming call, then Hendry's. From the beach-level observation post it looked like a fog rising from the water. From our higher level it looked like a spreading shadow, but there was not a cloud under the moon. A lone plane came over and dropped some brilliant parachute flares opposite Limay, about a thousand yards out in the water, seemingly as direction lights to guide boats.

Then the observation posts began to report they could hear considerable noise on the water but could see nothing. A thought occurred to me and I started to say, "That looks like . . ." just as Bonner said, "Could that be . . ." and we both yelled, "Smoke." A grab at the phone and in a few seconds the searchlights hit the cloudbank. Smoke it was. Three boats in a diamond point were moving slowly to the southwest, angling for the shore near Limay, building up a heavy smoke screen behind them.

It was almost windless, and the smoke hung on the water in a heavy mass. However, in the screen's edge and extending several thousand yards back we could glimpse many vessels. I believe the Japanese miscalculated the distance to shore, as they had done on previous nights. If the smoke screen had been laid about a thousand yards from shore, it would have been a fine cloak for the infantry-laden boats. Instead, it was well over six thousand yards out.

As soon as our searchlights picked up the screen, the wooden battleships opened up, and from within the smoke many large and small craft turned and started directly toward shore. In addition to heavy detonations, there were many sharp barks of lighter tone indicating the presence of the infantry pack cannon; tracer ammunition disclosed heavy and light machine guns.

This was our first experience in plotting the location of targets while using searchlights, and we quickly found we needed better coordination. I wanted to get an intersection on the leading vessel, the middle, and the rear. But the searchlights played up and down the line of boats, flipped on and off, and did not hold long enough on any one point for us to get a checked reading from our three observation posts. After a few minutes, I gave up and told the battalions to blaze away as soon as they thought the ships were within effective range.

By this time the smoke-laying ships were almost abreast of Limay, but the mass of boats had broken out of the screen and were heading toward shore about a thousand to fifteen hundred yards south of Pandan. The boats were continuing a brisk fire but only a few shots reached shore, falling between our guns and the East road.

Standing there I felt a strange sense of relief. After all the weeks of preparation, working, driving, cheering, cajoling, wondering, and fearing, the test was at hand. The attack was coming at the point at which we were best prepared. It had been launched too far out, and the element of surprise had been lost. I had done all I could do. The action was now in the hands of the young men in the junior ranks. I was a spectator —a stage director watching the first night from a seat in the balcony—and a beautiful spectacle it was. The powerful lights flickering on the crest of the wave ripples, already mirrorlike under the bright moon, re-reflected a thousand times. A million little mirrors on the caps of the ripples shot lights back, making clear definition of the vessels virtually impossible. The tracers and gun flashes, all behind the heavy pall of the smoke screen, made a pageant like a super-duper colossal movie.

Our guns opened up. The next day Hendry told me that

they had misjudged the range, opening at four thousand yards and getting shorts. They got overs at forty-five hundred yards, held there a while, then began to get both shorts and overs. As the boats began to withdraw the bracket center moved to five thousand yards, then fifty-five hundred. At that range the fire ceased when the boats pulled back into the smoke screen.

The engagement lasted just a little over an hour. The boats had not been able to get closer than four thousand yards. McKee was furious that they did not come within infantry range, but I was satisfied.

The next morning I went to the guns and did some back-patting. All of the gun crews thought they had inflicted tremendous damage. Catalan and I did not. The unusual light had made positive range sensing difficult, and the movement of the boats made many direct hits unlikely. From our observation post we had not seen anything we could describe as a hit. Some bits of debris, a few life preservers, many smoke cans, and two life rafts drifted ashore, but no bodies.*

We ironed out the difficulty with the searchlights. We established that they would pick up a boat, flip their lights in a pre-arranged signal, and then darken. After a short period, to let the observation posts get set, they would light, pick up the boat, hold for twenty seconds, and then darken.

I was interested in the improvised smoke cans that floated in. A five-gallon kerosene can had been emptied and soldered tight to make it float. To it were wired four cylinders that looked exactly like our four-inch-diameter tin map tubes.

---

*Some bodies did drift in several times while we were on beach defense. They were Filipino dressed as fishermen with their hands and feet tied. They had many bayonet wounds and seemed to have been dead when thrown in the water. It was my belief they were agents, or suspected agents, employed by the Philippine army G-2. There was a steady flow of such agents throughout the campaign bringing us a great mass of irrelevant information ranging from the suicide of General Homma (who was very much alive when we surrendered), to the establishment of 2,000 planes at Clark Field (which had a capacity of about 100), to the price of Camel cigarettes in Manila.

These cylinders contained the smoke compound and a rather crude wick. Most of those that drifted ashore were only about one-third burnt. Obviously improvised, they nevertheless provided a good heavy screen.

I expected there would be another attempt the following night, with the smoke laid closer to the shore. I exhorted the crews to alertness, but it was unnecessary.

The attempt came as I expected, but on this night (April 5 to 6) two of our China river gunboats had left the shelter of Corregidor, slipped along the Cavite shore, and cut in behind the wooden battleships. We were spectators to vivid exchanges of bursting shells, machine-gun tracers, and a regular Fourth of July barrage of skyrockets, but the action was close to the Manila side of the bay and so we were quiet all night. Firing continued spasmodically most of the night and, just before dawn, the two gunboats eased in close to shore and went south to Corregidor under the cover of our guns.*

Although we did not know it, our beach action was finished. From April 5 on we were more concerned with support of the front line than with the beach. During the 5th the aerial bombing of the East road area and the beach artillery positions intensified and, as I have mentioned, the hostile penetration west of Mt. Samat assumed alarming proportions. I was called to corps and told to leave the southern battalions on beach defense, using the guns of the two northern battalions to support the front line. Since this had been our contingent mission for some weeks, there should have been no question about it, but when I checked the alternate positions, I found they still required some cutting to fire as far west as I expected action to take place. I visited Colonel Irwin to coordinate the artillery with the infantry and learned that there was no pressure on his front worthy of the name, that Subsector B was dropping back to the upper portion of the trail leading to the San Vincente, and that

---

*These vessels were the river gunboats U.S.S. *Mindanao* and either the U.S.S. *Oahu* or U.S.S. *Luzon*. —Ed.

he was refusing his left flank along the upper section of the Patoc trail to conform and holding his right on the East road. A severe bombing of Lamao and vicinity on April 5 destroyed one of our searchlights, caused many infantry casualties, and practically wiped out a gun crew of Battery E. Although there were forty or fifty bomb craters in the vicinity, the principal damage was done by one supersize bomb. Its crater measured 120 feet in diameter, the largest I saw during the entire campaign.

Lieutenant Corleto, commander of Battery E, requested and received permission to move one platoon to an alternate position. Pressure of other matters and my confidence in Savoie caused me to neglect it, but after the platoon was moved I visited the position. It was entirely satisfactory except that the assigned mission could not be fulfilled from it. While I was there Catalan and Villa-Real also visited it. They felt the position was not the best, but that no better one existed in the area. They emphasized that Savoie had picked it and obviously relished my embarrassment at having to criticize him. Because I had an urgent appointment at corps, I asked Catalan to have a thorough reconnaissance of the area made for a more satisfactory position and move the Battery E platoon to it at once or else reoccupy the old position.

When I returned from corps, the platoon was still in the unsatisfactory position without orders to move. I made a personal reconnaissance and found a suitable position—one which in fact enfiladed the entire Lamao beach and was exactly what we wanted. At the CP I learned that Catalan had likewise found the good position but saw no reason to occupy it. I asked Colonel Daugherty to visit both positions and, after a look at both, he gave Catalan a direct order to occupy the better location as soon as possible. There was time to do so before dark, but night fell with the new position unoccupied.

The next day all hell broke loose, and I do not know whether the move was ever made. This incident was the straw that broke the camel's back and led directly to Catalan's relief.

Before daylight on the 6th, I talked by phone to Daugherty, who said the situation was grave and told me to go to corps headquarters for a conference. General King was present at this midmorning meeting at Luzon Force CP, where corps had moved. He asked what percentage of effectives each unit commander had. Someone asked him what he meant by "effective." He replied that an effective was a soldier who could walk with his weapon one hundred yards without stopping to rest and who could still shoot. The replies from units still cohesive showed fifteen percent of our strength effective under King's definition.

The decision was made to order all troops to reform on and hold the line along the San Vincente River. This was a naturally strong position, and there was a reasonable chance the enemy attack could be checked there.

Possibly I have created the impression that the Japanese attacks met little or no resistance after the initial penetration. That is not true. It is true that lack of communication and reserves prevented an orderly, coordinated resistance. But there were many gallant, heroic actions. Some individuals and units became panic stricken when they found the enemy infiltrating their flanks, and ran. But there are many who stuck, fighting desperately, dropping back slowly and stubbornly; many who stayed by their guns—and who are still there.

The enemy had no walk-through. They had to fight for every foot. In prison camp we were told by Japanese veterans of Malaya and Singapore that their fiercest resistance was encountered on Bataan. It took them about five days to drive their way around and across Samat to the commanding ridgetops, although they were opposed only by scattered bands of troops.

It was corps' hope to reform these small remnants at the San Vincente, giving them tanks around which to form combat groups and SPMs to provide mobile artillery support. Engineers from the trails of Bataan were being collected as combat troops, and so were the Americans of the supply services. The 31st Infantry (Philippine) had been little engaged and the Philippine 2nd Regular Division not at all. My artillery regiment was intact, as were three battalions of the Scout Artillery and the bulk of the 155-mm. howitzers.

If the tidewater section of the old line could be held, if the hostile attack could be stopped on the San Vincente, it was possible that a counterattack could be launched across the face of Mt. Samat and, in conjunction with an attack by I Corps down the Pilar-Bagal road, retrieve the situation.

I was ordered to use at least two battalions to support Subsector A, Colonel Irwin commanding, and at the same time to keep an eye on the beach. I was authorized to use my judgment as to which action to support in case of an attack upon both the front and the beach. I was likewise authorized to withdraw all the artillery under my command south of the Alangan River when, in my judgment, an attack down either Trail 10 or the Damalog trail would jeopardize us. Further, in the event of withdrawal of the Subsector A troops, I was to conform—an indication that corps did not have much hope in a San Vincente action being successful.

After visiting Irwin's CP on April 17, I went over the situation with my battalion commanders and instructors and Villa-Real, who had that day resumed duty as regimental executive (he had been the provisional battalion commander and, incidentally, had received his majority February 8). We conferred at the CP of Lieutenant Colonel McKee, commander of the 31st Infantry's 2nd Battalion.

My instructions were for the 1st Battalion to abandon beach defense, aim its guns to the north instead, and support Irwin. The 2nd Battalion was to remain in beach defense positions, with trucks at the guns, ready to move to direct support positions only a few yards away. Both battalions were to maintain constant liaison with Irwin and give him any support he desired, instantly and without question, while maintaining motor and foot patrols well up the Damalog trail and Trail 10 to keep an eye on the hostile situation there.

Both battalions were also to reconnoiter at once for positions on the south bluffs of the Alangan River. I was fully aware that these bluffs would probably become the infantry front line and that my guns there would come under small arms fire. But if conditions so deteriorated that the infantry withdrew to the Alangan, it would be a last stand, with no time to consider safe, normal artillery positions. The infantry would desperately need artillery support, and it would have to be given under direct fire conditions. The guns might serve as rallying points for the infantry, and, if they were sacrificed, it would only be a few hours earlier than we would lose them anyway.

If communication remained intact, I was to be kept in touch with the situation and would give any orders for withdrawal. If contact with me was lost, the battalion commander could withdraw if that was approved by the instructor. Any guns having to be abandoned would be destroyed.

Villa-Real was directed to locate and prepare positions for the 3rd and 4th Battalions in the vicinity of Lamao, from where they could support the Alangan line. But events moved too fast, and this was not done.

While our conference was going on, McKee's area was subjected to heavy aerial bombing, and many of his installations were blown out. Afterward, a phone call from our 2nd Battalion informed Harrison and Mercado that their sleeping dugout had received a direct hit, and they would no longer have the inconvenience of moving their personal belongings about. Earlier, a shell had hit their command dugout, destroying all the fire-control equipment and the telephone switchboard.

After two long drinks of Scotch—my first since January—from a bottle produced by McKee's adjutant, I returned to our regimental CP and found new orders from corps: the San Vincente line would not be held; the infantry of Subsector A would withdraw under cover of darkness to the line of the Mamala River, and the artillery was to conform.

Around midnight Daugherty phoned me with still new orders. Now the Mamala line would not be held. The line would be organized instead—as I anticipated—on the bluffs south of the Alangan River. All artillery was to be placed south of Lamao before daylight, and I was to report to the corps CP as soon as my guns were safely there. The artillery mission would be indicated later; the immediate requirement was simply to get the guns south of Lamao.

Until an artillery mission was assigned, it was obviously desirable that we cover the infantry on the Alangan pending other orders. It was with this in mind that I had directed Villa-Real to reconnoiter for positions south of Lamao. He had been unable to do this, and I could not censure him for it. Things were moving too fast; our communication and transportation were too disrupted.

After talking with Daugherty, I ordered the 3rd Battalion by telephone to abandon beach defense, swing the guns north, use the remnants of our beach defense phone system to establish liaison with Irwin on the Alangan, and prepare to support him. Since we were not in telephonic communication with the 1st and 2nd Battalions, they were issued orders by messenger to withdraw to bivouac south of Lamao. Except for the three or four days my guns were in bivouac just after entering Bataan, this was the only period of the entire campaign when they were not either in battle position or changing position.

I directed that the CP be moved at once to some location near Cabcaben. It didn't make any difference where it was located, since there was no phone wire and no possibility of an organized setup—I merely wanted to get it and its collection of pleasant young men the hell out of the way.

There was considerable delay in getting this move started. Catalan objected to it on the basis that Garcia was not going to move. I pointed out that Garcia had an infantry unit and might well stay where he was or even move forward, but that all of our guns had been ordered south of our CP, and, while there had been a number of times when I had wanted our CP to be closer to battle, this was certainly not any time to have chaplain, doctors, motor officers, messes, cooks, and other household personnel between our muzzles and our enemy.

But although I fussed and fumed, it was several hours before Catalan was ready with the command car. We even had a hot breakfast: cracked wheat mush, sugar, and condensed milk. It was the last hot food—almost the last food—I was to taste for six days.

We finally started just after dawn, passing on the way the last guns of the 2nd Battalion moving south. The other two battalions also had moved, but the 4th (Provisional) Battalion with its 2.95-in. howitzers and naval landing guns had not yet started. Since it had no motor transport of its own, we had to hold this battalion in position until the other battalions had moved and could send trucks back for it. When we arrived at Battery G, the guns were limbered up but carefully tucked under trees because the bombers had arrived and were laying eggs all over the Alangan bluffs. As the planes circled away, we would send out one truck at a time. All were finally out, and Catalan and I followed as far as the position of one of the emplaced three-inch submarine guns. I personally destroyed this weapon.

Although the 4th Battalion's move took place entirely in daylight, and the column of individually moving trucks was bombed repeatedly, every gun got back safely, and casualties amounted to only a few wounded.

I must praise the work done by our truck drivers and ammunition men during this movement and those of the next two days. It always took two or three round trips to move the regiment with its ammunition. At this stage of the game it took even longer, since so many of the old cripples had fallen by the wayside, we were down to few vehicles, mostly the bare gun trucks. These shuttled back and forth as fast as they could, un-loading and returning for another load. It was seldom possible to get all the ammunition and impedimenta to the rear in ad-vance of the guns. Thus, a final trip back to the old position, after guns had been withdrawn, was always necessary. The spot-bombing tactics made it impossible to send trucks in convoy. Each driver was on his own—running when he could and hitting the ditch when the planes dropped down. With the location of the front line indefinite, the infantry disorganized, snipers throughout the area, artillery constantly interdicting road junctions, and under unremitting bombing, the trucks made their repeated trips. We destroyed some ammunition—abandoning a little, I regret to say—but every movable gun and eighty percent of our ammunition reached the position of our final action—a fine piece of work by our drivers.

On the way back to corps to get orders, I stopped at the 3rd Battalion. It had not yet moved or established liaison with the infantry on the Alangan. The driving force of Savoie was miss-ing, and nothing was being accomplished. I left Villa-Real there with some of the regimental staff to form an advanced echelon of the regimental CP and went on with Catalan to report to Daugherty. The other artillery commanders were already there.

The conference was lengthy. Catalan left before it was over to organize the CP near Cabcaben. It finally ended with the following information and orders, excerpted from my notes:

"The infantry situation is obscure, very disorganized, and very fluid. The enemy has reached the junction of Trails 6 and 8 and has forced General Lough and the troops remaining of his original subsector to the west into the area of the I Corps. The troops remaining to the II Corps will hold on the follow-ing lines if ordered withdrawn from any more advanced line:

"a) the Alangan River;
"b) the Lamao River;
"c) the Pias River.

"The only artillery remaining to the II Corps consists of

four battalions of the 21st Field Artillery, three battalions of the Scout Artillery, and three guns of the 301st Field Artillery.

"The 4th Battalion (Provisional), 21st Field Artillery, with the fixed naval guns will take over the defense of Manila Bay.

"The organic three battalions, 21st Field Artillery (Colonel Mallonée), will support the right half of the defensive line (Colonel Irwin). . . ."

This order, issued at 11 A.M. April 8, was the last I ever received for the employment of artillery in the defense of Bataan.

During the return trip to the regiment, we ran into one of the most severe bombings I ever experienced. A mass of infantry, almost entirely stragglers, was caught on the open road by a flight of bombers. The casualties were heavy. We were in the middle and had to make a wild dash to get out.

I reached the 3rd Battalion CP shortly after noon and issued orders for the occupation of the Lamao bluffs. The 3rd Battalion would hold its position and the 1st would occupy the bluffs west of the East road north of Lamao. The 2nd Battalion, in general support, would go in astride the road and behind the other two battalions. The 4th would occupy beach defense positions north of Bataan Field.

I was displeased that the 3rd Batallion had not yet established an observation post on the Alangan bluffs or established liaison with Irwin. I was given the excuse that we were in telephone communication with Colonel Garcia, who was still at his CP barrio. Again I cursed the politics that had deprived me of Savoie. I tried to get across to Villa-Real and Acosta that we wanted someone on the front line who could conduct fire, not someone miles deep in the jungle in a hole; that Irwin was in command, not Garcia; and that the excuse for failure to establish contact and get into action smacked of cowardice. The ball started to roll then.

To ascertain the front line situation, I went forward with Bonner to find Irwin. The bombers were working the road again and it was a shambles, choked with refugees, military and civilian. Hardly a hundred yards was without its ditches lined with dead. One bomb hit near a running soldier, and when the smoke settled only the torso was in the center of the road. Bumanlag had to jerk the wheel hard to avoid running over it.

I found a rear CP of the 31st Infantry (Philippine) in the old motor pool near the Lamao docks, but Irwin was up on the line. Bonner and I continued forward and met a jeep with Lieutenant Colonel McKee, Captain Lawton, and Captain Forinash. McKee was white with anger. He told me that the infantry line, including his beloved 31st, had disintegrated under heavy bombing. He had reached the Alangan River position early in the morning with about twelve hundred men and occupied it in good order. Three waves of bombers hit: in midmorning, shortly before noon, and shortly after. By the third attack the twelve hundred men had dwindled to about four hundred and the officers could not hold them. By 3 P.M. there was no semblance of a line on the Alangan River. McKee estimated that his men had not suffered more than fifty to seventy-five casualties, mostly wounded.

He, Irwin, and the other officers were rounding up men, forming small groups, and sending them to the line of the Lamao, where they hoped to get a sufficient number formed to go back to the Alangan.

We found Irwin and listened to him tell corps by phone that there was no line on his front, and—what I had not known— that the troops of the 2nd Regular Division on his right, occupying a position from the East road to the beach, had likewise vanished. Furthermore, he had been unable to contact any troops on his left. Irwin was told by corps that the provost marshal was gathering stragglers near Cabcaben, so he started there to collect as many men as he could.

I arranged with Irwin and McKee to send a liaison officer to the bluff of the Alangan River, and about 4:30 P.M. I returned to the CP of the 3rd Battalion south of Lamao.

I was concerned that once again the muzzles of my guns were the front line, with no infantry in front of them or on line with them, but I was not unduly alarmed for there had been no enemy contact on Subsector A. There were no sounds of firing in that area. Even the planes had let us alone for the last hour or so.

We agreed the best we could do was stay there, get our observers forward, register each battalion upon the bluffs north of the Alangan, be prepared to fire at dawn, and hope the infantry could be reformed during the night.

I decided to try to get something to eat at the regimental CP, but, for the first time in the war, Bernado, my cook, was sick and there was no food. While the orderlies were trying to stir up something I went on to corps. There I learned that the situation was very "fluid." General Lough, with the 45th Infantry—the combat unit formed from the engineers—and remnants of two Filipino regiments were trying to recapture the junction of Trails 6 and 8, but nothing definite was known of their success or failure. There were sounds of fighting on the north Mariveles slope, but nothing was known about that either. The provost marshal had succeeded in collecting stragglers, refitting many, and had formed a unit that was to move forward at dusk. Colonel Irwin had been back collecting the 31st Philippine; the scattered remnants of the 31st American had reformed and possibly were the troops in action on the Mariveles slope.

I returned to our CP near Cabcaben. Some cans of food had been opened and were being heated. I was destined not to get that meal. As I had returned from corps, I noticed that southbound traffic had increased but thought nothing of it. Suddenly, down the road came the unmistakable rumble and rattle of the wooden-wheeled gun battalion. I was on my way to the road when an officer of that battalion came in and with the unfailing courtesy of the Filipino said, "Good evening, sir. How are you this evening?"

"What the hell are you doing here?"

"Sir, I have the guns of the 2nd Battalion here with me. Where should we go?"

"What in the name of Almighty God are you doing with the guns back here?"

"Sir, the Nipponese have landed at Lamao and Major Villa-Real ordered all guns out of position. I heard you were here and decided to report to you. Captain Mercado is at the rear of the column."

Thirty seconds later we were on our way north in the command car, leaving someone, I don't remember whom, to get the guns off the road and under cover and await orders.

As we fought our way forward against the mass of traffic— more vehicles than I thought were left on Bataan—fear clutched my heart. If the enemy had landed at Lamao, I had guessed wrong, there had been no land action, and my guns had been swung landward, leaving the beach open.

As we worked our way up the column, I questioned every officer I could see and soon found that the enemy had not landed at Lamao. In fact, there had been no action on the East road at all. The whole thing was obscure, but if any Japanese had come in they came from the mountains, not the water.

Then we found Villa-Real, who had little more information than I had received on the way up. About an hour after I left him, an American colonel came through the CP and told them the Japanese were entering Lamao and that all artillery had been ordered out of position to a new rendezvous. Heavy firing had developed south and west of the guns—behind them— and was getting closer. Everything was quiet in front, but there was as yet no contact with the liaison group. Villa-Real waited until the guns of the Scout Artillery moved southward, past him, and then gave the final withdrawal order of the war.

The 3rd Battalion now went into position near and south of the 1st. From long habit I checked the guns that passed me. One gun of the 1st Battalion was missing and no one knew where it was. Then I remembered I hadn't seen Captain Hendry and asked where he was. Oh, yes, they remembered. One gun at Battery A—the last one out of position—had motor trouble. Hendry had stayed with the gun and its crew and told the others to send a truck back. But they had not been able to do so, and now several hours had passed. Heavy rifle fire had come from the moutain south of the spot where the gun had been left, and it seemed certain that its crew and Hendry were now dead or captured.

Hendry, Harrison, and Savoie had become as sons to me. When I learned Hendry had been left behind, there was no question in my mind as to my course of action. I asked for someone who knew where he had been left to volunteer to go back with me. Lieutenant Clemente immediately volunteered. I asked Harrison to drive and suggested to Catalan that he remain and get the guns into position. Bonner asked to be allowed to go along. Four of us made up the party: Bonner, Harrison, Clemente—God bless his stout heart—and myself.

Just north of Bataan field, we ran out of the southbound traffic and from there on saw no one. About two kilometers south of Lamao we heard what sounded like ammunition dumps exploding, followed by gunfire from the area west of the road that I think was hostile.

We reached the bluffs safely and, turning west for a kilometer or so, found the crew, its gun, and Hendry. He told this story.

As the truck was pulling out of position, the driver from the corps pool deliberately rammed it on a tree stump, tearing the crankcase out. The driver took to the woods. Hendry waited with the crew for a relief truck, which he had ordered to return when the others got two kilometers south, intending to shuttle two guns with one truck in two jumps. He could have saved himself and the crew by climbing on another truck, and later could still have gotten out on foot, but he elected to stay in the hope of saving the gun. He had just decided to try to work south on foot when we arrived.

The story should have had a happy ending, but it didn't. We couldn't get the gun out. We hitched the trail lunette to the command car pintle, but the pintle was defective and we couldn't go five yards without the gun jumping out. We wasted more than thirty minutes before deciding to abandon it. Hendry destroyed it after salvaging the sight, setter, and breech block.

We loaded Hendry, his ten men, and the four of us on the command car and started out. Bonner had Harrison's tommy gun, I had a Garand, and all the gun crew had rifles, so I felt a little easier going out than I had coming in.

We went cautiously until we hit the main road and the area of the small arms firing, then Harrison gave the old boat hell. We came through advancing Japanese elements on both sides of the road. They were firing sporadically, but I think entirely at shadows.

It was almost midnight when we got back to Cabcaben. The traffic was still jammed tight from Cabcaben Field south. Catalan was waiting with a message for me: report to corps CP without delay. There was no possible chance of getting a vehicle through that traffic for hours; so, leaving Harrison to bring the command car along when it was possible, I walked the five kilometers. I was dead tired and damned near done in when I arrived. Daugherty asked my situation and told me to sit tight for orders. I sat, or dozed, from midnight until about 2 A.M. with some other officers. Then suddenly a violent earthquake had us holding on to our shoes. It was followed by a telephone call at 2:15 A.M. advising us to take cover because the army ammunition dump was to be blown up. For about an hour there were violent explosions—four so severe the earth trembled for several seconds before we heard the sound. There was no cover; we could do nothing but hit the dirt while fragments whistled around us. A few moments before 4 A.M. the telephone ring we had been awaiting was heard. Daugherty gave us our orders, word by word, as they came over the phone. "Destroy guns, ammunition, and material before 7 A.M. Cease all destruction and further hostilities as of that time. Form in units, without arms, on the nearest road at that time. The army is surrendering as of 7 A.M."

Harrison had joined me a few minutes before, bringing the command car. We went out to the East road where he had left Catalan and Villa-Real. I repeated the orders.

It was impossible to buck the Mariveles-bound traffic with the car. I couldn't have walked a hundred yards. I hadn't slept since before the last wooden-battleship attack on the 6th or 7th, and hadn't eaten anything since the porridge of the 8th. I suddenly felt let down, very old, and very tired.

Fortunately, Catalan and Villa-Real knew where the guns were and started for them on foot, with orders to destroy them before 7 A.M. now about two and a half hours away.

A nurse in a group along the roadside appealed to me as I sat there waiting for a chance to get the car into the stream of traffic flowing against the way I wanted to go. She was one of a group of seven or eight nurses who had been left behind by transportation, which was supposed to get them to Mariveles before midnight—now long past—to take a boat to Corregidor. I took them as far as Base No. 1, where I saw some medical vehicles and other nurses, also Mariveles bound. The nurses with me joined them.

Making way slowly against the traffic, I reached our CP just before 7 A.M. En route I saw the end battalion guns, well destroyed—tubes split and fire-blackened. From Villa-Real, Catalan, and the battalion commanders, I received official reports that every gun of the regiment had been destroyed.

We had a quick breakfast of cold canned beans and canned tomatoes, and I opened the warm bottle of champagne I had carried throughout the campaign to celebrate the arrival of the relief expedition. Bonner, Hendry, Harrison, Catalan, Villa-Real, and I pledged each other in a wordless toast.

With a last hand clasp and tears in my eyes, I said good-by to my companions of the campaign—Catalan, Villa-Real, Bernado the cook, Datoon my orderly, several officers of the staff whom I dimly saw through my tears and cannot remember—and then the American officers left in conformity with orders to report to corps CP for formal surrender. I left behind me fine memories, dead in the ashes of our lost cause, but retained lasting pride that I had participated in the campaign with the finest artillery regiment in the Philippine army.

From the moment I had listened to the radio of the news of the attack on Pearl Harbor—December 8, 1941—four months and a day had passed.

3

The Death March

I know of no event in history that parallels, much less exceeds, the catastrophe of the evacuation of the surrendered Bataan Force from the southern tip of the peninsula — the evacuation that has become known as the Death March.

The Japanese had no organization to effect that march. It all had to be done in haste. Time was a major factor. The Japanese had to get troops into position in the area where we surrendered for the assault upon Corregidor. Also, we wanted to leave behind that disease-infested scene of our humiliation— and this desire was accelerated when the Corregidor guns opened up on the Cabcaben area while our columns were on the march there.

To repeat, the Japanese had no visible organization. Bataan was a swarming mass of dirty, tired, hungry, sick, bewildered Americans and Filipinos—although most of those adjectives can be applied to the Japanese as well.

General King had tried to persuade the Japanese to allow him and his staff to form our units and move us in an orderly fashion, using our own vehicles to the extent possible, and assembling us at any point designated by General Homma. Col. Motoo Nakayama, Homma's operations officer, brusquely refused. In fact, he refused to accept the surrender of the Luzon Force as an entity. We were to surrender as individuals and as units, in his words, "voluntarily and unconditionally."

None of us knew at the time that the Japanese had a plan for prisoner evacuation. It was not until the war crime trials, which resulted in Homma's execution, that its existence became known. It is interesting to compare that plan with the ghastly events.

In March Homma received his reinforcements, troops brought back from the Australian and Burma-India theaters, and began preparing for his Good Friday offensive. If that offensive were successful, the Bataan Force could be expected to surrender, so Homma appointed five officers to plan for the prisoner evacuation. They were: Maj. Gen. Yosikata Kawane, transportation; Col. Toshimitsu Takatsi, administration; Maj. Moriya Wada, assistant to Takatsi; Maj. Hisashi Sekiguchi, in charge of medical affairs; and a first lieutenant in charge of a well-digging detachment that would provide water for the prisoners.

On March 23, ten days before the Good Friday offensive, this plan was approved by Homma and published in orders two days later.

It had two phases. The first, under the direct control of Colonel Takatsi, was to assemble all prisoners at Balanga by marching them there in the most direct route from their point of surrender. No food or water was to be provided during this phase, for it was expected to be completed in a day or less. This was the first point of breakdown. Even under the best of normal conditions, the march could not have been accomplished in that time. The second was to form prisoners in units and move northward from Balanga to a POW camp in central Luzon. Rest areas, sanitary facilities, water stations, kitchens, food stores, and other supply depots were to be stationed at short intervals along the route. Hospitals were to be set up at

Balanga, Lubao, and, if one arrived from Japan in time, at Orani. The planners expected they could move about one-fourth of the prisoners by motor vehicle. Priority was to be given to the sick, the walking wounded, and the weak. This simple plan conformed generally to the Geneva Convention, but it had no chance of success.

The first error of the planners was their estimate of the number of prisoners. In January Japanese intelligence estimated our strength at 40,000 to 50,000. In March, after casualties and sickness were considered, the estimate presented to Homma was 25,000. He refused to accept it and it was revised to 40,000. After our capitulation, Tokyo radio announced that 40,000 had surrendered. The early release from Washington announced the surrender of 36,853. Much later this was revised to 78,000 troops, 6,000 civilian employees (who had been rushed to Bataan to build the defensive positions), and 26,000 civilians who had scuttled into Bataan ahead of our withdrawal. So the Japanese estimate of 40,000 was about one-third of the actual number.

The next Japanese error was their failure to realize our poor physical condition. His intelligence informed Homma on January 7, two days after our half-ration order, that we had gone on these rations and were eating only two meals a day. It just didn't register.

The Japanese plan apparently was based upon marches of about twelve-and-a-half miles a day. In our condition such marches were impossible without collapse and death. Yet we were driven not only twelve miles a day but much longer. My group was marched continuously—with only short halts while we were still held in formation—for twenty-two hours, during which we covered forty-four kilometers.

At the war crime trials, Homma displayed his ignorance of our physical condition and food shortage, stating that if he had known of these, he never would have ordered the Good Friday offensive that took such a toll of Japanese, but would have awaited our white flags of starvation.

The final Japanese planning failure pleased me greatly. Homma had such a high respect for our combat effectiveness that he estimated it would take a month to knock us to our knees. He had been kicked in the teeth so hard during three months of combat that he expected more of the same. Therefore, General Kawane didn't hurry his plans for rest areas, stocking food supplies, and digging wells. So the Japanese had a deserved complaint against us. We didn't cooperate. We surrendered in five days instead of thirty, and the enemy wasn't ready.

Much has been written about the Death March. There have been accounts of atrocities, of massacres, and of men buried alive. I will not say they were not true, but, in the main, the horror of the death march resulted from the physical condition of the men forced to make it. The death toll was heightened by the Japanese failure to provide water, making it necessary for us to use any water available from streams and ditches along the route—nonpotable water that later caused further debility, illness, and death.

Top all this with the burning hell of the tropical heat and humidity, mix in the callous harshness of the Japanese, and you have the Death March.

After the events described in the final paragraphs of "Four Months and a Day," I returned to Cabcaben for the destruction of the guns and to say farewell to my comrades of the 21st Field Artillery.

Col. Alex Quintard and a few of his officers came to the CP. No food had been issued, and we ate from a few cans I had in my car. Several alarms occurred, and in the middle of the afternoon the first of the Japanese began to advance through our area.

I had been told to use my private car for the march out, carrying as many fellow officers as I could. That was a laugh. The Japanese would hardly allow us to tool merrily up the roads; besides, I had less than a gallon of gas and there was no more available.

I concluded that the march would be on foot. I only too well knew my physical condition and had stripped down to what I thought were the barest essentials. I carried one extra uniform, one change of underwear, two pairs of socks, and my toilet articles. In a shoulder roll I packed a blanket, a poncho, a change of underwear, a pair of socks, and a pair of shoes.

I made a bad mistake in neglecting to change my brimless overseas cap for a fatigue hat or sun helmet. I was to pay dearly for that mistake as the Filipino sun fried my addled brains, the glare making my eyes ache and burn.

At daylight on April 10 we had our last breakfast together—twelve or fourteen of us sharing one can of tomatoes, a small can of corned beef hash, and a four-ounce can of chicken sandwich spread.

In the middle of the morning, we received instructions to collect all American officers except the organic corps staff and proceed to a casual camp near Mariveles. Mariveles was south and west on the way to Corregidor. That gave rise to the first of many rumors that were to plague us for three-and-a-half years: President Roosevelt had ordered Wainwright to surrender Corregidor, but the condition was that we would be collected at Corregidor and held there until ships could come to return us to stateside.

We started out in cars but, as I had anticipated, we had a very short ride—less than two hundred yards—when bayonets were on all sides of us. We were dismounted, formed in a column of fours along the roadside, and searched for the first of a good many times. My shoulder roll was taken and never returned. As things turned out, I would not have had the strength to carry it anyway. But the loss of the shoulder roll cost me the almost-new shoes I had wrapped in the blanket. I was to pay dearly for that loss.

While at the roadside, we were looted by Japanese—both officers and men—who took anything that pleased them. About the only thing they left were items engraved with the owner's name or initials. Evidently, the penalties for proven looting were severe. Thus, I retained my Parker pen throughout the march and later in prison camp.

By the middle of the afternoon we were joined by other officers from corps and headquarters, Philippine Department. Finally we were moved to the main road and turned south toward Mariveles. After marching about a kilometer, we were halted for some time, then turned around and counter-marched toward Cabcaben. Apparently, the Japanese didn't know what they were doing. The road was badly congested. Our column was swollen with many others. Tactical organization did not exist and no American control was permitted. Some columns, like ours, had guards. Others had no guards and moved as they saw fit. In addition to the columns of prisoners, thousands of Filipinos, both soldiers and civilians, milled around during the evacuation from the battle zone. Columns intermingled and paralleled. Long halts were necessitated at bottlenecks.

In addition to all this there was a constant stream of Japanese troops moving south. Most were infantry: very hot, very tired, very dusty. One Japanese soldier seized my canteen for a drink and then started down the road with it. I gave chase and grabbed it back from him. He took a swing at me with his rifle butt but missed. A Japanese officer shouted at him and he went on down the road. That was the only incident I saw on the entire Death March in which a Japanese officer exercised restraint on his soldiers. If I had known at that moment what I learned in the next hour or so, the soldier would have kept the canteen. I did get it back, but many were not so fortunate.

The dust cloud was heavy. We breathed it, tasted it, swallowed it. The scorching heat, our hunger and weakened condition, the strain of the past four months, and the tension and anxiety of the past five days were already beginning to take their long toll. Many men collapsed as early as that first afternoon, principally personnel from the rear depots who were unaccustomed to physical exertion.

Having been a horse-drawn artilleryman, I was interested in the columns of Japanese artillery that shoved us into the ditches when they passed. The artillery animals looked in good flesh, well groomed and well handled by the drivers. Their harness adjustment was excellent. They looked like competent battle-trained combat units. Their pack trains were not in such good shape, the animals showing many sores and poorly adjusted loads. I was surprised at the paucity of motor equipment. Almost complete reliance was placed on horse transport. Many artillery pieces were being rushed forward, towed by or transported in trucks, but as we moved northward the next few days, we passed horse-drawn limbers and caissons moving south to rejoin the guns.

Many of the trucks we saw were American, and some were being driven by Americans at bayonet point. As one of these passed, it went out of control into the ditch. The door sprung open and the American driver fell out of the cab. The Japanese shouted at him, slapped him a couple of times, and then brought a gun butt down on his head. He did not get up. An officer nodded to a soldier who used his rifle butt some more —and the American never did get up.

Just about dusk we reached Cabcaben, where I was fortunate enough to get my canteen refilled. There, one of the most horrible things I have ever witnessed occurred. One of the Mexican soldiers (from the New Mexico antiaircraft unit) went crazy, shouting at the top of his lungs, beating the ground with his hands, striking his head against the side of a truck, jumping into the air. To the Japanese it was a spectacle. A group gathered around him, laughing. While thrashing around, he struck an officer. In a fraction of a second he was pinpointed by ten or twelve bayonet thrusts. After he fell in convulsions on the ground, he was bayoneted again and again.

I was not the only one who vomited. We marched long into that night. I had no conception of time because, after the first shakedown, I had destroyed my watch. Before we stopped, there was an angry shouting of Japanese officers, and our column was reversed and returned a kilometer or so toward Cabcaben. We joined a large column that had fallen out in a bend of the road which formed a large amphitheater sloping toward Manila Bay. We fell out and slept there probably until about 2 A.M., when we were formed in columns and moved northward again.

About dawn we reached what I knew as Bataan Airfield, where we were counted into units of 500 and moved northward. There was no organization. While some units were going north, others were fighting for the road space to move south. My column reached Limay about noon on April 11 and was formed in a close mass in the schoolyard. We were held there for several hours while being systematically searched. This was done under orders, and the searchers knew what they were looking for. They went through every pocket and into our shoes.

The sun was terrible as we sat there for several hours. There was a pump just outside the schoolyard, but we were not allowed to get water. A few men died there.

About midafternoon we were formed again. Field grade* officers and captains were trucked to Balanga, reaching there before dark. Again we were searched, with attention being given to small items, although very few of these had been overlooked by the previous searchers. Flashlight bulbs and batteries, automatic pencils, sunglasses, mess-kit knives, and razor blades were taken. One officer was beaten badly because he protested the loss of his prescription sunglasses.

We were held at Balanga for about an hour while, directly across the road, a Filipino column was being fed rice. Finally they finished and moved off. We were told to form fours in a field across from the kitchen. We thought it was for rice, and

---

*Majors, lieutenant colonels, and colonels are "field grade"; lieutenants and captains are "company grade."—Ed.

many left their musette bags and shoulder rolls where they were. Instead, we were put on the road north.

Gen. Albert Jones, I Corps commander, joined our column at Balanga with some of the I Corps officers. This was quite a surprise, as I thought the Japanese would move the corps commanders, if not all the general officers, by car. General Jones was an object of curiosity to the Japanese, the soldiers fingering his insignia and buttons. Jones was with us that night on the march to Orani, but I did not see him again after Orani until we arrived at O'Donnell.

We took the road to Balanga at 6 P.M. April 11 and marched continuously until 4 A.M. April 12, when we reached Orani. We were put in a wired compound, moved up tight—chest to back and elbow to elbow—and told to lie down and sleep. We got down to the ground somehow or other, legs spread, the man in front backed up against you, and you backed up against the man behind, and that is how we spent the night. Exhausted, acutely thirsty, stomachs rebelling from lack of food for several days, with aching muscles, raw blisters, and throats coated with dust, we were almost at the limit of our endurance. Many, as we found when morning came, had passed the limit and were gone. The two dead in my immediate vicinity had to be hauled out of the compound, and I have no idea how many more there were scattered through the group.

Over everything was a horrible stench. In the morning light we discovered the reason. The latrine trench provided for thousands of prisoners was an open pit, already overflowing with excreta and slime, and for several feet on each side swarming with gray, wriggling maggots.

During the morning, ten men at a time were taken out of the compound, each with ten canteens on a pole, to get water. I was fortunate enough to be one of them and was able to drink my fill and even splash my head and shoulders at the pump.

At the pump a Japanese officer told me in broken English, "No more marching. Go truck." We heard this all the way

along the route but put it down only as an attempt at rough
humor. During the day, tremendously hot with a blistering sun,
another officer and an enlisted man just a pace or so away
from me died.

We stayed in the overcrowded, filthy compound all day.
Those who had blankets or shelter halves stretched them along
the fence, and those of us who could crawled into the small
areas of shade. The effects of the march the night before made
me realize that even my half-filled musette bag was too heavy
for me. I threw away the extra shirt and trousers and gave the
change of underwear to Ralph Hirsch. That left me with the
clothes I had on, my mess kit, and toilet articles.

Twice during the day we were fed unsalted rice, about a
half canteen cup each time. We moved off again about 6 P.M.
April 12. This was to be the longest and hardest march of the
entire trek—the one that very nearly did me in and caused our
highest casualty rate.

I had put golf spikes in my shoes—wonderful for crawling
around in the jungle. Somewhere above Orani the road changed
to gravel. In the darkness I could not keep my footing on loose
gravel with those spikes. I stumbled and pitched and lurched.
Regaining my balance each step was a major effort. Several
times I fell. Finally I became delirious. Someone in the column
had a canteen banging against a piece of metal. It sounded
exactly like a bellboy coming down a hotel corridor with a
pitcher of cracked ice. But he never arrived. My friends told me
that I raved at that bellboy for miles. Harrison took my musette bag and carried it himself. When it got too heavy he threw
his own away. He was in almost as bad shape as I, but he had
one distinct advantage—youth. Finally my eyes wouldn't
track. I saw double, my legs gave way, and I fell. Harrison and
Hendry, they told me later, tugged me into a ditch where I lay
while the long column passed. Just before the guards at the
end reached me, they came across Col. Jack Irwin.

Harrison and Hendry got me on my feet, and, as I staggered

on, I heard a half-gasp and then a sound like water being sucked out of a half-stopped sink. It was Jack Irwin being bayoneted as he lay on the ground. Halts on this part of the march were irregular. Sometimes we would go for an hour without a halt, sometimes four hours. At the first halt after the Irwin incident a driving rain hit us. In a twinkling we were sopping to the skin. This rain was God-given; there is no question that it saved my life. The cold, biting shock of the water gave me new vigor.

After the rain we moved on, kilometer after kilometer. Several times we saw bodies beside the road. When we halted for a short time in Lubao, a Filipino interpreter very surreptitiously gave me a banana and a can of sardines. En route from Lubao to San Fernando, I was able to buy from a roadside stand a couple of mangos and a half dozen duck eggs. The column arrived at San Fernando at about 4 P.M. April 13, having been on the road for twenty-two hours and having covered forty-four kilometers. On the outskirts of San Fernando we passed a control booth of sorts. There the Japanese had an American colonel tied to a post with his arms strapped above his head. He had been badly flogged with straps or canes, and his back was a mass of welts.

We were impounded in the schoolyard at San Fernando and given one helping of rice. It was there to my surprise that I found Lieutenant Aquino. He gave me another mess kit full of rice and some vegetables.

The worst of our march was over, although we did not know it. We had marched one hundred seven kilometers in seventy-two hours with only one real rest—the fourteen hours in the sun on the baked ground of the Orani compound.

At 4 A.M. April 14 we were marched to the railroad station at San Fernando and loaded into boxcars, one hundred to the car. I sat with my back against Budge Howard's chest, with Harrison wedged between my legs. The car doors were closed. Had it been daylight, in the sun, only a few would have survived. We were detrained at Capas sometime after 6 A.M., and after a long wait we were marched about seven kilometers to Camp O'Donnell, arriving about noon.

The Americans knew that camp as O'DONN ell; the Filipinos knew it as o'dun NELL. We all knew it as Hell Hole No. 1.

It had been one of our training camps but was abandoned before the war because the water supply was inadequate for 8,000 men. Now it became the first POW camp, and into it went the Bataan Force—anywhere between 40,000 and 60,000 half-starved, emaciated, exhausted men, many already afflicted with cholera, dysentery, or other diseases.

Upon our arrival, we had a long wait in the sun and then were stripped and searched once again. All remaining personal possessions were confiscated—nail files, nail scissors, razors, blades, matches, penknives, cigarettes, pipe tobacco—along with all blankets, shelter halves, and rain mats.

The camp commander gave us a speech, and we were marched into the wire-enclosed stockade and halted. The guards left; apparently the Japanese intended us to come under the command and administration of our own officers. But while General King and members of his staff had preceded us by car or truck, as had a few other fortunate officers and men, the Japanese intention had not been communicated to the general. So we sat and fried for another two hours. We asked for water, but there was none; all water came from a single pump that was operated only two hours a day.

I passed out from the sun. When I came to, I decided I would rather take a chance on being shot than continue to bake, so I crawled into some available shade and went to sleep. When I awoke the column had been dispersed. Ed Williams fed me a few spoonfuls of beans from his last can of C rations and General King's aide gave me a few mouthfuls of water.

I finally found Bonner and the others. They had saved a spot for me in the building to which they had been assigned. It was a room nine by nine. In it were Bonner, Hendry, Harrison, and four other officers. The eight of us sardined into the cubicle by overlapping our legs.

Camp O'Donnell was our lowest ebb. The many rough experiences of the years ahead could not approach the despair of O'Donnell. I have known men decorated for less courage than that required to endure the daily life there.

The food at the camp consisted of *lugao* twice a day. *Lugao* was a watery gruel made from rice, half rotted before the cooks got it, into which were dunked a few putrid camotes, a type of root barely fit for animal fodder. There was no salt. There wasn't enough water to wash the kettles after each meal, and even if there had been, there was no soap.

To obtain drinking water, it was standard procedure to stand in line for six to eight hours for a canteenful from the single pump. The Japanese finally permitted the pump to operate full time instead of only two hours a day, but frequently it was broken down for longer periods than it worked.

Water was also obtained from a river about a mile away, but it was even worse. The river was about four inches deep—slimy mud into which the overflow of the pit latrines seeped, with only a scum of water on top. This water was nonpotable and had to be boiled. We sent a water guard of ten officers morning and afternoon to keep order at the river and prevent the men from drinking its water before it was boiled. But many men would leave the line, drink from the river where they could not be seen, then get back in line for more. Hundreds became diseased from this.

A fact impressed on me at O'Donnell was that the heaviest death rate from illness during the Bataan campaign and the POW days occurred among the youngsters, the recruits, and the civilian army, both officers and men. The old-timers had a big difference in our favor—water discipline. We had years of training and experience in getting along on a minimum of water and in avoiding contaminated water at all costs. The young men had never learned to deny themselves anything, and bad water killed them by the hundreds.

Thousands died at O'Donnell. From the beginning the rate was more than one hundred a day. Soon it reached about twenty American and one hundred fifty Filipino lives a day. It became increasingly difficult to find and detail each morning those who had the strength to bury those who had died during the night.

Latrines were dug and filled the same day. It was common to collect the day's dead from around the latrines each morning. This was because men with dysentery tried to sleep near the latrines, and the bodies of those who gave up during the night were found there at dawn.

I found out one thing at O'Donnell: when a man doesn't want to live it is pretty easy to die. Many gave up and did just that, although suffering no more than the rest of us. Others, like Luther Stevens, you couldn't kill. We left him behind almost dead two or three times when we changed camps, but he was still alive and kicking at the end.

The building I was first in was later made into a hospital. We were moved into one of the barracks, a double-deck bamboo affair. There were sixty of us in that building. Still later, all colonels were moved into what had been the regimental recreation hall and chapel. Finally, we were told on May 8 that all generals and colonels were to be transferred to Tarlac. I was loath to leave Bonner, Hendry, Savoie, Harrison, Ganahl, and the others, but I was not my own master. God only knew what was ahead for us. Yet we could all hold our heads high with what little strength we had remaining. We did everything possible, and more. And it was primarily the Filipino who deserved credit. He showed himself, even when half starved, able to match and beat the cream of the battle-seasoned Japanese forces. If only the United States had started the training programs and material buildup two years, even one year, earlier, the outcome could have been so different. The Filipino simply did not have enough time.

Even so, many had become superb fighters. I have no doubt that many of the future leaders of the Philippines were forged in the fires of Bataan.

Mabuhay to you, my Filipino compatriots. I hoped the months ahead would be less grim for them than they promised to be for me.

4

Guests
of the
Emperor

May 10, 1942. The trip to Tarlac filled me with very mixed emotions. We passed Capas junction, where I waited in such agony of mind for the arrival of the 2nd Battalion; where Sergeant Crabbe of Lieutenant Day's SPM platoon had so effectively used the butt of his pistol upon glaring headlights; and where Harrison's platoon had covered the beach approach. We traveled along the road where many times I had played hide and seek with Herman; we passed the division CP where Montgomery had given us the distressing news that D-5 was to be abandoned as a final defensive line in favor of the Bataan retirement. We drove by the San Miguel Hotel, where Catalan, the battalion commanders, and I had lunch on the occasion of our inspection trip to our Sta. Ignacia camp. The building was still standing, but with doors ajar and windows broken—a hollow shell without life or movement.

We skirted the hill where Fisher's battery had been posted, near the canefield line from which the 2nd Battalion had fired when they debouched from Tarlac. I could see the area of the 1st and 3rd Battalions where we had our first fire fight on

land, and where we had written glorious history. We crossed
the bridge over which the tanks and Lieutenant Day's platoon
had tried to escape. I looked for signs of the vehicles to see
whether we had been able to destroy them or not. Nothing was
visible. The vehicles had been removed—as had the countless
buses and trucks the North Luzon Forces had abandoned all
along the road—removed to become metal junk. I still do not
know the fate of the tanks.

Our convoy was taken into Tarlac and then back along
Route 15 to the cadre barracks. When I last saw it, Tarlac had
been in flames as a result of aerial bombing. Now the damage
did not appear very great. The marketplace showed signs of
fire and bomb damage, as did several buildings, but in the main
it was not greatly changed. The main street presented about
the same appearance, except that about two-thirds of the shops
were empty and had not resumed business. Many market stands
had mangos, eggs, bananas, coconuts, canned goods—the many
things we had been craving since our early days on Bataan.

Our barracks were filthy—left so by the previous users.
There were no brooms, cloths, water, or other cleaning mate-
rials, but we did the best we could. Double-decker iron beds
with wooden "mattresses" were available, and we were given
one blanket, one sheet, one very small dollsize pillow, and a
mosquito bar, all hard used but better than nothing.

The soldier orderlies supposedly assigned to the officers
actually became the camp slaveys, servants for the Japs, strong
backs to do the dirty jobs of the camp. Not that the lot of the
officers improved to any extent, either. For all of us, it remained a grim inhuman existence.

Rough as it was, with harsh treatment, horrible sanitary
conditions, an almost complete absence of medicines, a sort of
hit-and-miss schedule of food, Tarlac was still a vast improvement over what we had left behind at Hell Hole O'Donnell.

The evening before I left O'Donnell I had had an attack of
dysentery. Harrison gave me three sulfathyazol tablets, which

helped a lot. Nevertheless, I had to stay in bed except when en route to or from the latrine pits about a hundred yards away. We had no water for the flush toilets.

May 13, 1942. I was still sick and took four sulfathyazol tablets which Glately, the MD, was able to buy at the Tarlac civilian hospital, where he had taken General Stevens. Stevens was in a bad way and was not expected to live to leave O'Donnell.

While the food at Tarlac was basically *lugao* and *camotes*, at least the rice was not spoiled, not moldy. Occasionally, we got additional items, purchased for us either by the Japs or by our own mess people with the little money we had when we reached the POW camp.

Infrequently, we actually got meat, though barely enough to flavor the soup. Every now and then there would be a banana or half a mango. One time we got two pounds of coffee—two pounds for the 120 of us. I know that it will be most difficult for you to believe me—in fact, it seems almost impossible—but that two pounds of coffee, eked out by charred rice brewed with it, had a strange effect upon those grown men, senior officers. There may have been just enough caffeine to produce the effect, or it may have been purely psychological, but in their weakened condition, about half the group got as high as if they had drunk several Scotch and sodas. Old army songs were rendered in barbershop harmony. Impromptu jigs and square dances shook the building. The Interpreter came running, fearing a riot. He sat there for over an hour, incredulous but highly amused. After it wore off there were, incredibly enough, many hangovers.

Regulations were put in effect by which we had to salute all Jap officers and sentries.

A small goat made the mistake of wandering into our compound. It dressed to fourteen pounds. We had a nice goat flavor in our soup and even got a few shreds of meat—about one-half can of delicious soup per man.

We also bought one *balut*,* one-and-a-half bananas, and one-and-a-half teaspoons of soy sauce per man.

The commandant of all the POW camps in the Philippines was Colonel Ito. He was a friendly, human sort of person—all terms being relative, of course. On one occasion, he made us a gift of some cookies; on another, of some sugar. Nothing like that ever happened after we left Tarlac.

From our first few days at O'Donnell, we had heard rumors that we were to be exchanged for Jap nationals in the States, that the president had directed Wainwright to negotiate the surrender of Corregidor on the basis of our being turned loose, and many other rumors, equally silly. The optimists were kidding themselves and were woefully ignorant of the slowness of diplomatic machinery. Before we parted, I had told Bonner, Hendry, and Harrison that if there was an exchange, which I could not envision, it would take until October or later to effect it, and that if MacArthur, through some strange miracle, was able to assemble a striking force of sufficient magnitude to warrant the offensive, we could not be cut out before Christmas. But hope persisted, and so did the rumors. (We were to be subjected to hundreds of them in the years to come.)

Dinty Moore gave me a razor and two blades which he got in some fashion from the Japs at O'Donnell. He also loaned me one of his two pipes. The one I had left, after giving one to Daugherty, had disappeared on the march. (So my diary states. Actually, it was thrown into the jungle by a vindictive Jap.)

Our lives at Tarlac soon settled into a general routine. We rose, put our quarters in shape, washed and shaved if enough water was available, ate breakfast, and then did various tasks such as washing, mending, or altering our clothing. After lunch

---

*A *balut* is a partially developed fertilized egg which has been allowed to "ripen," generally by placing it in the ground for several days or so. It is a Filipino "delicacy" most Americans prefer to shun, but we were glad to get them.

we generally played cards, listened to rumors, stood for inspections (which seemed, in the years to come, to be almost as numerous as the rumors), or just sat and talked. I often wrote in my diary. We welcomed the change in routine of new prisoners coming in or of a new rumor from a Filipino driver who brought in supplies.

Sunday, May 17, 1942. Saturday I had a sad, sad birthday.* My entire celebration consisted of smoking one of my carefully hoarded cigars—and of my memories. We had no news since our capture except that of the fall of Corregidor.

I drew a job as water corporal. Water was a major problem. We were on a pipeline from Tarlac. The pressure was low and only at certain times did the water reach us. When it did, we filled oil drums for reserve supply: kitchen water, drinking water, wash water, laundry water, and toilet water—in that priority. The toilet water was used for the flush toilets—if we didn't have it, we had to use the slit latrine. My job was to see to the filling of the drums in the proper priority.

Tuesday, May 21. Food was the subject of paramount importance. The menu for one day consisted of rice and salt at night, rice and one tablespoon of sugar in the morning, and rice, a teaspoon of shredded coconut, and a mango at noon: the latter, a result of our own purchases. My digestive tract was almost back to normal.

That evening we had fish chowder, made from two pounds of dried fish, similar to our "dead fish" of which I am so fond at cocktail time. The result was just juice, of course, but it flavored the rice. The next morning we had rice and sugar, then we had four days of nothing but rice.

A Jap officer, reputed to be the colonel in charge of our district, visited us. He walked into the mess hall where some men were playing cards. They did something wrong; presumably,

*The author was forty-three years old.—Ed.

they were slow in coming to attention. He tore up the cards and disciplined the men on the spot. A long confab with General King followed. We did our best to observe rigidly the rules and regulations given us, but there were many ground rules with which we were not familiar.

The sick list was high—nine out of seventy-five—but only two seemed serious. Dysentery, malaria, and weakness were the common complaints to which were added later respiratory troubles, when the rains hit us in full force.

Wednesday, May 27. While our clothes dried on the line, we were turned out for an inspection by Colonel Ito. He spoke to us in English—the first time anyone had done so, except through an interpreter—telling us to observe the rules, admire the scenery, and safeguard our health.

Rumors of the collapse of Germany persisted.

We had a mango with our *lugao* for breakfast, but no sugar.

A thought occurred to me last evening. I remembered that Mama always used to urge food upon us—pickles, preserves, jams, jellies, and more of the main dishes—usually with the expression, "Eat plenty, children, there's more in the kitchen." From my experience in Tarlac, I felt certain that this desire to have everyone eat heartily had its inception during the Civil War and the Reconstruction days, when there definitely was not plenty.*

The soles of my shoes were separating from the undersole, so I sent them in for repair. They came back tacked instead of sewn. Since there was no chance of getting other shoes, I didn't know what I would do when these went. My money was about gone. I was weak, tired, and mentally low.

Monday, June 1. Malaria finally caught up with me. I had a light touch on Friday and a real heller on Sunday—chills and a

---

*"Mama" Mallonée, born in 1850, was Colonel Mallonée's grandmother. A product of the Civil War and the Reconstruction, she died in 1933, so even her great grandchildren remember her "eat plenty."—Ed.

high fever. The medico said it would recur every other day, and that I would have a tough one the next day. It wasn't too good getting it where I had one blanket, one uniform, and nothing to change into when I got soaking wet after the fever. At least the medico had some quinine.

At the peak of the fever, I thought of iced orange juice, ice cream, and the other things I would be getting had I been in a stateside hospital. The food had not been too good for a few days, but Sunday one of the men on detail brought in a chicken, which was stewed for the sick. It was a delicious broth with a few shreds of meat. Last evening our purchases got us twenty-five chickens and some hard-boiled eggs. I had a hard-boiled egg that morning. It was ancient and pretty powerful, but I forced it down for the badly needed protein. We got the chickens that noon.

The main thought of most at Tarlac was simply to get home. I was constantly irritated by the lads who were planning to get soft cushy jobs at ROTC* or other country-club assignments in order to coast out the remaining years of their service. The loudest were those who were most conspicuous as not being worth a damn when they were needed—the coasters of the last twenty years. God knows, I wanted to go home, but not if there was a job still to be done. If, however, I was forced to retire physically, that was another matter. Then, I did not know what I would want to do eventually.†

We were again on water rations, with the supply always uncertain. From the day I left Honolulu, water everywhere had been short—and bad. The malaria was still with me. My ears

---

*ROTC, or Reserve Officers Training Corps, generally is a college assignment.—Ed.

†After Colonel Mallonée returned to the States, he served as post commander of Fort Bragg, North Carolina; post commander of Fort McPherson, Georgia, then Third Army Headquarters; and finally, post commander of Fort Monroe, then headquarters of CONARC, Continental Army Command, before retiring.—Ed.

rang from quinine and I was as deaf as a post, but all in all I felt better.

Thursday, June 4, 1942. The Japs ordered us to move our double-deck bunks closer together (leaving twelve to fourteen inches only) and to remain inside. About thirty officers had just arrived and were outside going through the customary speechmaking and search. They were the generals and colonels of Corregidor, under General Moore. General Wainright followed a few days later. From what little we could see of them as they marched in, it looked as if they, too, had been pushed around a lot. While the last days on Corregidor had been almost as rough on them as the last days of Bataan had been on us, they had had no Death March. In addition, they were lousy with baggage which the Japs trucked out for them—suitcases, valet packs, trunk lockers, and bedding rolls. Some owners were stingy with their possessions, but those Corregidor bags helped most of us. In my case, Tom Dooley and Bob Brown gave me a shirt and a pair of pants. By that time my rear end was waving in the breeze.

The Corregidor people dispelled our hopeful rumors of a negotiated surrender, under which we would all be released, by telling us that Corregidor was taken. But they brought many "hope" rumors including Germany was near collapse, Russian forces were on German soil, Hitler had fled, thousands of Anglo-American planes were over Germany daily, 400,000 American troops were in England for a definite second front in France, Russia was at war with Japan, six Japanese cities were being bombed daily, Japanese Diet resigned, MacArthur had retaken New Guinea and Java, and Japan was asking for a ten-day armistice to discuss peace terms. Their actual reliable news was not much different than what we had heard at the date of our surrender.

Another rumor was that Russian nationals in Manila were being interned. We hoped that these were all true, but to me they sounded like the wildest of dreams.

Stu Wood went to Australia by plane from Corregidor at some point in the last few days. Some doubted if he had got past Mindanao. The American death list at O'Donnell had reached 1,060, with the Filipino rate up to 400 a day.

A group came in from Bilibid, including several naval officers—one line, one supply, three medicos, and two marines. Their news of the Coral Sea battle and that of the Bay of Bengal was most encouraging. I had about concluded that Japan could maintain the status quo, even with her far-flung line, until the German situation permitted the full American fleet to be employed here. Their news gave me hope that, even with the major portion of our fleet employed on the Atlantic convoy, we might have sufficient strength to whittle our opponents down little by little.

One of the signal officers from the Rock told me of receiving a technical radiogram from Australia signed "Autrey." He was with an army signal unit, so maybe Dutch Kreuger and the Third Army were there. I hoped so. If Dutch Kreuger was there and they gave him a couple of rowboats and a free hand, he could be on Luzon soon. However, Autrey may have come over as an individual, not with a unit. We could hope though.

Monday, June 15. Our oldest son's birthday. I wondered if he was at home and whether my wife was making him a cake. We had so much time to think and remember. Waiting for the morning roll call, I thought of crisp bacon and eggs on toast. I must have moaned out loud at the recollection, as my neighbor asked me if I were sick—I was, at heart, over all this. I had done my part—and had done it well. More I could not do, nor, if I had been Napoleon, could I have averted this tragedy. Our whole situation was so futile.

The ration yesterday brought us another live pig. We got little or no meat from the pig among the 180 of us, but it gave us grease, a flavor, and some protein.

We were given a propaganda newspaper telling of an overwhelming Japanese naval victory at Midway, an attack on Dutch Harbor (in Alaska). The conclusions drawn were that the American navy was destroyed or impotent and that the Pacific Coast and the Panama Canal were open to attack, I read other things into the newspaper as well. The admitted losses were two aircraft carriers—one sunk, the other heavily damaged—and one damaged cruiser. An interesting item explained that their navy could accept a ship-for-ship loss with us because, considering the distribution of our fleet, they had more than we had. This was false reasoning, of course, and I supposed that they had had heavier losses than they wished to think. We heard that KGI gave their losses as three battleships, three aircraft carriers, one heavy cruiser, one transport, several sunken merchant supply ships, and five damaged cruisers. But the big thing was that they finally were checked, our navy was at last functioning, and Midway was again in our hands.

The ration truck came in, but the rations looked like rice and fish heads only. The fish heads were pretty hard to stomach, but we had to eat.

I had been trying to work out a way of getting some of my extra clothes from the trunks I put in storage at the beginning of the war, but my efforts were fruitless.

We were beginning to get crabby and crotchety from too much close association with each other. Minor trifles magnified, nerves grated.

I had access to a *New Testament* but would have liked to have had an *Old Testament* also. *The New Testament* leaned so much to "love thy neighbor," "turn the other cheek," and "forgive thy enemies." I believed in it, but I would have liked the comfort of *The Old Testament* warriors who, with His assistance, wreaked the vengeance of God upon their enemies.

Wednesday, June 17. New prison camp rules: up at 6:30 A.M., formation at 6:40, and breakfast at 8:00. Evening formation was at 8:00 P.M. and thereafter we were not allowed to sit outside of the barracks—not allowed to sit outside until the lights went out as before. Smoking out of the barracks was prohibited, except at one designated place, and only then with an ashtray in reach.*

---

*From then on smoking restrictions became more onerous. The Japanese had an inordinate fear of cigarettes causing fires.—Ed.

A Filipino shoe man was allowed in to take orders for shoes. I needed them badly but had no money. I also could not afford more razor blades and started growing a beard. Saturday, June 20, 1942. We had pig, rice, and gravy. The pig had a peculiar taste. I hoped it was okay. It must have taken at least 200 years of careful inbreeding to develop a pig as tough, greasy, and tasteless as the swaybellied Filipino pigs.

By the next day we knew the pig had *not* been good—about one-third of our group, myself included, had a violent case of food poisoning. The MD shot a big dose of soda water into me to wash out my stomach by induced vomiting; this was followed by a bismuth and pepsin pill and then salts. We were all straightened around today but naturally much weaker from the experience—and I didn't have any strength to spare.

One day we were inspected by Colonel Ito. There was a Lieutenant Usi with him in American-made riding breeches—sans boots.

We heard rumors of several guerrilla raids against town garrisons.

Sunday, July 12, 1942. Fourteen colonels arrived from Bilibid, Wood and Brezina among them. So Stu Wood didn't make it out. Too bad! The rains came. We then had an epidemic of respiratory troubles in addition to the dysentery and malaria.

Jack Vance had the latrine cave in under him, dropping him into the pot. Fortunately, he caught the edge, or there might have been another tragedy. As it was, we had a digging party to make a new latrine.

I had a short talk with Stu Wood who thought our action over here would be minor until Germany was beaten. His opinion was of value only if it reflected as a basis information he had access to while G-2; I doubted if he had very much. I, too, thought Germany would receive first attention but not to the complete exclusion of our major effort—but probably not for a long time. The first thing was to safeguard Australia and India. The prospects for our return were very remote; as a group, we were deteriorating rapidly—physically and mentally.

After all, we were but 14,000 Americans out of our army (which by then must have been four or six million strong). I doubted there were more than 10,000 of us left. The administration, looking at the big picture involving millions of men and thousands of miles, could have had but a passing regret for the unfortunate fate of the ill and starved 10,000. I hoped they even remembered that we saved Australia.

Of the approximately one hundred thirty officers here, I doubted if more than twenty could go back into action at once; these were mainly from the Rock and high command groups upon whom the physical and mental strain of the campaign had not been so great. Another fifty could go back after a month's rest, medication, and American food. The remainder would never do full duty again—they probably would not last through prison camp.* At least twenty, possibly thirty, should not have been in active service when the war started.

A medical rumor revealed that 20,000 Filipinos had died at O'Donnell—two out of five. It didn't seem possible, but they were going at a rate of 130 to 150 per day when we left.†

Friday, July 31. The "milk" was getting thinner and thinner —nine cans for twelve gallons of water. They barely colored the water—and woe on woe, when it was gone there was no more. No *camotes* or eggplants were issued, not even *gabi*, a tasteless sort of starchy nothing which gave some bulk. We had two days of rice; there was nothing in the pantry then but rice. Our breakfasts of *lugao*, milk-water, and purchased sugar were our best meals, except for the occasional meat meals which generally were once a week.

Wainwright completed forty years of service.

A small cow with a slight fever was brought in. The vet thought it would be okay if we waited until the fever subsided. When we did have it, the portions amounted to almost four ounces per person. My waist measured thirty-two inches and

---

*As unfortunately many did not.—Ed.

†At the worst it was 400 per day.—Ed.

my weight was about one hundred fifty. I had been holding my own for three months.

Sunday, August 9, 1942. There was great activity. On Friday, August 7, a Japanese lieutenant who had arrived several days before officially informed us that we would leave in three days for Japan or Formosa. On the same date we got a rumor of great submarine activity off Luzon, four transports having been sunk. Naturally, there was also a rumor that this move was a prelude to our exchange.

The Japanese doctors took blood and feces from us to test for malaria and worms. Since Bataan was full of malaria and ground worms, I supposed that most of us had both—but what they were going to do about it, I didn't know.

Tuesday, August 11, 1942. We were up at 3:30 A.M. and ate *lugao* and milk-water in the dark. We had heavy typhoon rains until 6:00 A.M., but it was clear for the trip to the railroad and we were thankful. We were formed and marched through the streets of Tarlac to the railroad station. It was obvious that there had been "No Demonstration" orders, for no Filipino uttered a sound. It made me rather happy in one respect, and very sad in another, to see the number of women in the throng who were weeping silently (and in the half shadows were holding up their fingers in the V-for-victory sign). No men! Presumably, their men were still at O'Donnell.

In the middle of one large group, a boy of about fourteen bravely whistled "Auld Lang Syne" while our column passed.

At the railroad station we were packed into third-class coaches, much to our pleasant surprise, instead of the boxcars we expected.

The trip to Manila caused me many heartaches, reminding me of the trips I had made along the same route in happier days. Upon arrival in Manila, we were issued bread and sugar, then moved by truck to Pier 7. There was very little movement

on the streets and none at all of motor transportation, except
for military.

We sat on the dock . . . and sat . . . and sat, sweltering in the
heat. We became dry with thirst. This was to become par for
the course.

Suddenly we were snapped to attention and, at bayonet
point, moved to one end of the pier, almost out of sight, and
made to kneel and bow our heads on the dock. We were kept
in that position for what seemed an endless time while the
Japs, with much bowing and scraping and with great pomp and
ceremony, carried little white boxes aboard the ship. The
boxes contained the ashes of cremated Japanese soldiers we
had killed while defending the Philippines. There were several
thousand, and this was only one of many ships that carried
the white boxes back to Japan.

We then loaded onto the *Nagara Maru*, a seven-to-ten-
thousand-ton freighter made in 1934. It turned out to be very
trim and fast—my guess was that we made about seventeen
knots most of the time.

We were put in the forward hold and were badly crowded.
Temporary shelves had been built with just sufficient head
room *not* enabling us to sit quite upright. We were sardined in
—fourteen to a bay.

Our heads were against the shipside. I was in the upper shelf
with my head only a few inches from the steel deck, which
was so hot we could not hold our hands against it. About dusk
we were allowed on deck.

August 12, 1942. We lay tied up to the pier all night of the
11th, moved outside the breakwater early on the 12th, and
dropped anchor—remaining there until the afternoon of the
12th when we sailed. It was timed so that we would pass out
of the entrance of Manila Bay after dark. We were all held below decks until we had passed Corregidor, but we did catch
sight of a destroyer and several other vessels with us.

That was the first of a number of similar voyages we were
to make as "guests" of the Japanese emperor. It was unpleasant and crowded, but, in retrospect, it was the best of our

Japanese conducted tours. We were allowed considerable freedom to roam on the deck at will. It was the only time such a thing ever happened. The weather was fine. There was plenty of water and a help-yourself cauldron of steaming hot tea, around the clock. The food was excellent, with fish, meat, many vegetables, seaweed, salted fruit, and all the rice we could eat. But this was the last voyage by ship, train, truck, or foot about which anything favorable could be said.

August 14, 1942. We reached Takao Harbor on the south shore of Formosa (Taiwan) in the early morning. It was a beautiful, landlocked harbor with a very narrow entrance. There were four or five large ships anchored in the roads, and many small ships were tied at the docks or were up in ways being repaired.

About twenty ships were in the harbor. There was a sister ship to ours, three or more ships around five thousand tons, and—a depressing sight—the *President Harrison*, which had been refloated after having been run aground at Shanghai. The rest were from one hundred to five hundred tons, very small.

We remained on board until the afternoon of the 15th, having had in the interim another rectal examination. We disembarked by lighter and were taken directly to No. 107 (the *Otaru Maru*). It was a small interland vessel—very filthy, very old—whose barnacled bottom should have been sent to its graveyard many years ago. It was such a poor ship no one used its name, only its number.

Rats infested the ship. McCafferty took his shoes off to sleep and had three toes badly mauled.

Karenko,* August 17, 1942. We arrived at Karenko in the morning but did not get to the pier to unload until noon. We

---

*Karenko was the Japanese name for the town known as Hua-lein by the Taiwanese and Chinese. It is a beautiful resort town located on the middle of the eastern Taiwan coast and is much favored by honeymooners. Nearby is the home of the Ami, an indigenous people who are world-renowned for their superb dancing and choreography. Ami teams have toured both Europe and the United States many times.

were taken to a warehouse, counted several times, and then turned over to a brand-new recruit guard. We were then marched about three kilometers—possibly four—generally along the half-moon bay, to the edge of the town, where we were turned into a large compound. There we were stripped to the skin and thoroughly searched. Our shoes were taken away from us and were not returned.* Clogs were issued in their place.

Our toilet articles and clothing were returned, but all else— notebooks, letters, pictures, razors and blades, and food items —were held for more minute search. None of our food items were seen again.

Then the Commandant, Captain Imamura (Little Snake Eyes to the prisoners), made a speech. Word for word, the interpreter's translation was:

"I am head of this prisoners' camp. Having received you here, I wish to instruct you as follows. The following are general principles which I require you to observe:

1. Anyone who does not observe the Nippon military discipline shall be severely punished. *And the life of such prisoner shall not always be assured.*

2. To be loath to labor or to express dissatisfaction for food, clothing, or habitation is prohibited. No Nippon, with the solid unity of one hundred million, is fighting against the United States and Britain with firm conviction of victory.†

There are no idle persons living in our country. Everyone in the nation is most patriotic and ready to sacrifice himself for the sake of *His Majesty, the Emperor!*

Everyone in the country is willing to endure all sorts of hardships and fighting for the final victory of war. You must understand, therefore, that it is nothing but natural that you will not be allowed to lead idle life.

---

*They were returned later with the heels cut away, presumably to prevent running in them if a prisoner tried to escape.—Ed.

†The confused verbiage of this translation, saying exactly the opposite of what was intended, was customary and on many occasions fouled up an already confused situation.

3. The Americans and English are not allowed to hold the haughty attitude over the peoples of Asia or look down upon them, which has been their custom for a long time. If there is any such attitude on your part you shall be severely punished.

4. The language spoken to you daily is the Nippon language. English is used only when it is necessary. You must, therefore, make diligent effort to understand Nipponese for your daily use.

5. If you obey the orders, rules, and regulations in this camp and put them faithfully into use, you shall be given just protection and be able to return to your fatherland when peace is restored."

We were then marched to dormitories—twenty-two to a room. We were issued four blankets, all cotton, two small sheets, one Japanese-type hard pillow, and a pillowcase. The next day we were redistributed in other rooms—still twenty-two in my room—and were issued a straw mattress, a mattress cover, and an iron bunk with iron strips crossing in about eight-inch squares.

The rules and regulations were explained to us in detail that afternoon. One we found out the hard way. All references were to be to *Nippon* or to the *Nipponese*. It would cost us a slap, or worse yet, a gun butt, to use the words *Japan* or *Japanese*. *Jap* was even worse.

Among many of the rules was the requirement that we come to attention and bow stiffly from the hips whenever a "Nipponese" entered our squad room or passed us anywhere in the compound, and whenever we passed a sentry on duty. This salute was to be given not only to the Japanese officers, but to every enlisted man.*

---

*Each Japanese military rank was required to do the same thing for every rank above it. Prisoners of war were considered to be below the lowest Japanese private. Every rank could discipline and punish the lower ranks for indiscretions. Therefore, every Japanese rank could discipline and punish any POW. Punishment varied from standing at attention for a given length of time, often in the direct sun, to cuffings, slappings, or the use of rifle butts, all administered immediately after the observed infraction. More stringent or serious punishment could be directed by the Japanese sergeants or officers.

Also, at a given order during morning roll call, we were to bow to a white stick in the eastern wall representing the Imperial Emperor, God of the Rising Sun.

Thursday, August 27, 1942. We had been in Karenko ten days and were getting fairly well shaken down. We were on the Japanese ration—rice and meatless vegetable soup—three times daily. We were told that we would get meat once a month, fish twice a month, and bread twice a month. The soup had new vegetables in it: some long root vegetable we called walking cane, a type of *gabi*, some very tasteless onions, and some others. I had never before tried boiled cucumbers.

In quantity we were getting much less than we had been getting at Tarlac, and I was getting very hungry again.

We awoke by bugle at 6:00 A.M., made our beds, cleaned up, and fell in for *bongo* (roll call by numbers) at 6:30. We were then required to bow to the east to the emperor, as exemplified by the sun. We were closely guarded at this formation, and the discipline was very rigid. We were given fifteen minutes for setting up exercises and then were dismissed to have breakfast at 7:00. We sent by roster officers from each squad to the kitchen. They returned with two wooden buckets, one containing rice and the other soup. This was distributed in the squad room. I supposed that when one was starving and there was little to do, thoughts of food became of prime importance. At any rate, there had been several childish squabbles over claimed unequal distribution—there was so little that the gut boys watched every grain of rice and every spoonful of soup. It had even reached the point where the clear liquid at the top of the soup bucket was distributed first, and then the few vegetables in the bottom were doled out. Claim was made that, if the soup was stirred, those getting the bottom of the bucket got a few more weeds and onion tops than the others—for that was about all the soup was.

Scenically, Karenko was a beautiful spot and our compound was a beautiful place. It had been a Christian missionary school but more recently a peacetime garrison for a battalion. It was much in the Chinese home-compound style. The grounds were well kept and the buildings were in good condition. For the only time in our POW experience, there was an adequate amount of water, delicious ice-cold water.

Karenko was on a shelf between the ocean and beautiful towering mountains just a few miles inland. So far the climate had been fine, more temperate than tropical. We were told, however, that it got very cold in winter, which would come all too soon.

In our compound there were many strange varieties of flowers and trees. Across the compound rose a stone with a terrace above it on which there were several houses reminiscent of the tea houses of the Peking Summer Palace. We could see the mountains rising eight or nine thousand feet to our west but could only hear the surf of the ocean. As we stood at morning roll call, we could just see a deep pink tint—very colorful—to the underside of the clouds to the east. Then suddenly the tops of the mountains to the west would be bathed in sunlight —beautiful. In peacetime this would have been a splendid vacation setting.*

But the beauty of our setting could not conceal the depths of our misery. We stayed long, bitter months in Karenko. Volumes could have been written about that ordeal. Our guards were Formosan soldiers who had been drafted into the Japanese army, but who had never been trusted enough to be sent into combat. They knew they were considered inferior, so they tried to show the Jap officers how good they were by being a little harder and a little crueler than the Japs themselves.

*Indeed, it was a splendid vacation site, at the Astar Hotel along the coast in Hua-lein. Incidentally, the compound was being used in 1971 by elements of the Republic of China army who allowed us to come into their administration building for questioning, but who were suspicious and eventually refused to allow us to examine the compound we had traveled around half the world to see. The glimpses we were able to get revealed that it looked the same as it must have when Colonel Mallonée was there.—Ed.

Chuck Lawrence was beaten into insensibility three or four times one afternoon by the mess NCO, and to this day no one knows what Colonel Lawrence did to infuriate the NCO, least of all Colonel Lawrence.

At seven consecutive morning parades, another colonel who had offended a guard was called forward and was made to kneel with his hands clasped behind his back while he was slapped six times, three on each check. They were not love pats; he was knocked over each time. By the end of the seventh day, his face resembled beef steak.

A civilian named Webb, a Red Cross official, should not have been in a POW camp; instead, he should have been interned. He protested this fact and got put in the black box several times for two days at a time. The black box was like a telephone-booth type—too small to lie down in, too short to stand up in —and had no latrine facilities. Shades of the Inquisition!

Hazing was the rule, especially at night when Japanese officers were not present. One of the guards' cute tricks was to hide in the shadows, near the *benjo* (latrine). A POW hurrying to the *benjo*, who did not see one of them and failed to make the bow of obeisance from the hips, would get slapped with the butt of a gun, or, more fun, would be made to stand at attention until nature could endure no more and the bowels would empty.

For the first time at Karenko, officers were required to do manual work in the fields. We were told this was "voluntary work" that would supplement our rations by the food we would grow. Those who at first refused, as I did, found themselves on half portions of the already inadequate soup and rice; within days, we traded our convictions for a hoe.

Sunday, August 30, 1942. Captain MacMillan, naval governor of Guam, arrived from Kobe. He said the Japanese authorities at Kobe admitted that they had lost fifty percent of their naval strength. He had to write an explanation as to why Tokyo had been bombed (twice)—our first news that it had been.

The latrine was an open, straddle-trench type, and the contents were removed at intervals for fertilizer by the bucket method.* When we went to the *benjo* after evening roll call, we had to go past it to a vigilante guard in the center of the building, give our name and room number, return to the *benjo*, then check back with the guard, and go back to our rooms. With our diet as liquid as it was, we spent a lot of evenings walking back and forth.

We were to be given an allowance of 310 yen per month, which we did not see. Two hundred eighty was to be placed on deposit in the post office for us, three would go to our enlisted men, and the remaining twenty-seven would be used to buy food and "things."

Wednesday, September 9, 1942. I still had dysentery and was not feeling well. The doctor gave me two morphine and two atrophine tablets which were the only type he had. Eventually, I got relief by sleep.

A group of sixty British, Australian, and Dutch officers arrived last night. It was a high ranking group: C. G. (Perceval) of Singapore, generals, brigadiers, Supreme Court justices, governors, and civil administrators. They told us of growing allied strength over here and of a second front in Europe. They were very confident. We were skeptical because we had been fooled many times, but we were always hopeful. After all, many of them were captured before we were.

Incidentally, the Japanese considered that the British at Singapore made a gentlemen's fight and then surrendered without either side losing face (to which the Orientals attach great import). For this they were allowed to bring their record collections, cases of books, and much other paraphernalia. Naturally, we benefitted greatly by having stories to read and music to hear.

---

*Even though it was inside the building.—Ed.

One of the Englishmen had a sense of humor which was very enjoyable. When finally we were allowed to write our first letters home, this chap quoted Imamura, saying that we could not speak about the living conditions. Likewise, we could not speak about our treatment. He continued, "The food is also unspeakable." It got past the Jap censor.

General Perceval, as the senior POW, asked for a conference with the Nipponese commandant to present the matters of insufficient food and rough treatment. He was informed that the commandant would not grant personal interviews, would not recognize rank among POWs, and would not receive complaints except in writing from individuals. If the complaints were decided to be unjustified, the writer had to expect disciplinary action.

Monday, September 28, 1942. The Mindanao group arrived Sunday night and were in five-day quarantine. They were Fletcher Sharp, four other generals, twenty colonels, and sixteen enlisted men.

One British officer was forced to kneel while having his face slapped repeatedly. Several were taken to the guard house, slapped repeatedly, then released.

The Mindanao group came from Cabanatuan. Winfield Scott died of malaria there: Bob Vesey and two others were executed publicly.

Sunday, October 11, 1942. We became so hungry we searched the grounds for snails. We got a bucketful which we cleaned and made into soup for the squad. They were rather tasteless and rubbery and did not have much food value, but they were something to eat for anyone as hungry as we were.

Sickness continued. Kohn had paralysis and nothing could be done about it. Stowell had an infected leg and was in a weakened condition that he couldn't throw off. There was the usual run of beriberi and sore legs and throats.

The weather became bitterly cold for us. The wind swept down from those towering mountains covered in sheets of ice and snow. Everything is relative. I didn't suppose the temperature ever dropped below 40° F., but there was no heat in any of the typical frame-and-paper construction buildings through which the wind blew all the time. Even if there had been a heating system, we would not have been allowed to use it— the Japs were scared stiff of fire. If we had had warm clothes, it might not have been so bad, but we didn't.

The rice was heavy with weevils and an occasional maggot— these added piquant, if undesirable, flavoring. Hungry as I was, my stomach refused snails after a while. They were too slimy.

November 11. Once, November 11 was Armistice Day, but no longer. That morning Major General Beckwith-Smith, B.A., died of diphtheria.

We were taken outside the compound each day to work. Then, we were spading up a garden between the compound wall and the river. We had prepared several acres, but there was still the rest of the island to prepare if they wanted us to.

December 5, 1942. It was bitterly cold, and we really suffered from insufficient clothing, cold drafty rooms, and no heat. The food was exceptionally poor and our suffering increased. We were back almost to the level of the days we had been coerced to work—we worked, but it hadn't done us any good. Even the gesture of work rice wasn't resorted to except occasionally—and then by shorting us for two days to make up for the work-rice increase.

Finally, we were allowed to purchase "warm" clothing—a blue cloth, corduroy suit pattern of an ersatz material which resembled wood pulp, or something like coarse jute. It wasn't very warm, but it was better than cotton.

December 25, 1942. Christmas morning. On Christmas Eve we had a little celebration. A group of about twenty-five of us—the choir—received permission from the authorities to walk around the barracks singing Christmas carols. We had decorated the rooms rather pitifully with colored strings made from cut-up cigarette and tea boxes. We cut out and hung up stars and triple candles, and I made Christmas cards out of cigarette boxes for the squad and placed them on the table. It was all well received. That morning we had a fine Christmas service conducted by General Perceval, with General King reading the scripture lessons of the birth of Christ. The choir sang Christmas hymns and carols—and I was very hoarse from the unusual strain of singing the night before and that morning.

Monday, January 4, 1943. It was a bad day in more ways than one. There was high, biting and bitter wind—a three-pants day. The squad room was very cold; everyone was half frozen and miserable, yet we were ordered out—lieutenant generals, governors, all officers except hospital patients and red cards— to clear ground for a farm. In our weakened, half-starved, sick condition it was terrible. Just the walk up the steep hill to the latest site was almost enough to do me in. Yet we were guarded by sentries with loaded guns and fixed bayonets. I remembered seeing similarly guarded prison gangs in the States, but I never expected to be in one myself. We came in exhausted to three-fourths of a cup of rice and a small portion of very thin soup, little better than warm water.

The reign of hazing had increased again. There were slappings and rifle butting, and the cold winds were up to forty miles per hour.

Tuesday, February 9. I worked in the morning wearing four coats and was stopped by rain in the afternoon. A rumor from a Nippon officer disclosed that twenty-two German divisions had surrendered at Stalingrad.

Tuesday, February 16. The letter home which Maher wrote last November had just been returned with orders to leave out mention of his weight. Three-and-one-half months ago and the camp censor had just read it! One of the most maddening things about our captivity was that we did not know whether our families knew we were alive.*

Sunday, February 28. A violent stomach cramp hit me. Manees had to take over the rice service for me. The pain sub-

---

*Colonee Mallonée's family did not know until the fall of 1944 that he had survived Bataan and was alive as of February 1943. See illustration of that letter.—Ed.

sided in the afternoon and evening. I was severely slapped in the evening for having a torn pocket, although I had submitted a request for thread for repair work three times. The stomach cramps hit me again the next day. I was in intense pain and in a cold sweat. The medical officer was afraid to give me authority to lie down unless the medical corporal approved—and the medical corporal was on pass. Bob Hoffman, who spoke Japanese fluently, went to the guard house to ask for permission, but the guard could not or would not give authority. Bob used the telephone to call up OD, who was not in camp, and caught hell for using it, although he did so at the direction of the sergeant of the guard. So I lay down on the floor until the violent pain subsided. This nonplused the guard who didn't know whether to allow it or not. When the medical corporal returned the next day, I was given a three days' rest card.

'The reign of terror increased. Berry and Lathrop were forced to hold water buckets at arm's length, with an upright bayonet just under their hands, which was withdrawn with great laughter just before exhaustion. Worse yet was having one's organs "stirred" with a rifle butt.

But one incident had a happier, if undignified, ending. Those who knew him will remember how thin "Skinny" Wainwright had always been and how bowed his legs were (as all horse cavalry soldiers' legs are said to be). Well, the enforced diet at our compound had made his legs look like a pair of badly warped pieces of bamboo.

While visiting the *benjo*,* General Wainwright failed to see and bow to Toad, a very loud and objectionable guard, who jerked him to attention, got his heels together, and then roared about his knees being apart, tapping them with his bayonet. Skinny got his knees together, but of course had to move his feet and then toe in. This caused another roar and his heels came back together as his knees spread. At this point Toad

---

*The version which follows was expanded by Colonel Mallonée from the diary to include remarks which *could* not be put in the diary.—Ed.

called the guard corporal and handed him his rifle. General Wainwright tensed, as this was usually the prelude to a severe beating. Instead, the guard knelt and held Wainwright's knees together with his hands to show what he wanted. As he removed his hands the knees bounced apart. Those who were there, also at attention, fully expected him to work Skinny over then.

Instead, a puzzled expression crossed his face. He again held the knees together. As he released them they again bounced apart. A pleased grin replaced the scowl. Even the corporal had to laugh. For the next five minutes or so, as a child would play with a jack-in-the-box, this moron played with the knees of the lieutenant general commanding the United States Forces in the Philippines.

Tuesday, March 16. The weather was overcast and damp, and there was no work. Again, I had a violent stomach attack in the late afternoon. Col. Paul Bunker died about 6:30 P.M. Disintegration caused by an improper diet was the basic cause. He was too weak to snap back from minor illness. From then on there were increasingly greater numbers passing away as disease and undernourishment combined to exact their toll.

Friday, April 2, 1943. All generals, British brigadiers, and civilian governors were moved to another camp.

Wednesday, May 5, 1943. Enlisted men went to another camp. I had a stomach ache and loose bowels. Five more in the squad had the same. Flies were over everything. The Japs started a campaign against flies. We were issued a bamboo split each and told to make a flyswatter. We saved the carcasses, counted them, and turned the bodies in to the Japanese. We killed from fifteen to eighteen hundred each day.

Menzie collapsed after having diarrhea for four days. Worse yet, Bob Hoffman, our only member fluent in Japanese, had a nervous breakdown. Day or night, when an irate guard started hazing us, we invariably shouted for "Ho-ma," and Bob came running to receive the full blast of the ire and to explain and

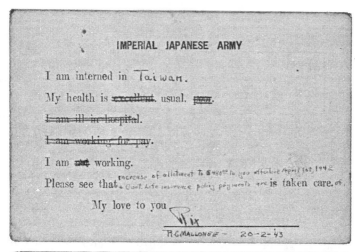

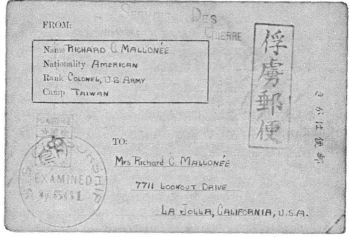

The above letter was the first from Colonel Mallonée to come out of prison camp. It was sent from Shirakawa, Taiwan. The characters are Chinese and state, "Taiwan, censored" with the seal of the censor therein, and on the right, "Prisoner of war letter." The French was applied by the international Red Cross in Switzerland and states, "Service for the prisoners of war." Sent February 20, 1943, it arrived the fall of 1944.

pour oil on the troubled waters. He had a fine, level head, good judgment, and an excellent way of placating the Japanese and of smoothing the road for us. He rendered invaluable service, and I wondered that he stood up under it so well and so long.

Wednesday, May 12. Hoffman was in bad shape. His mind was blank and he recognized no one. He needed a constant attendant; he had no balance and kept falling down and falling out of bed. It made me heartsick. (He eventually did recover.)

Thursday, May 20. I weighed 64.7 kilos—142 pounds—and had gained seventeen pounds since March 24. I believe this was largely the result of the Red Cross supplies, as the rations had been lacking in protein and caloric value since the potato crop gave out.

June 7, 1943. We moved to another camp. My marching baggage consisted of my blanket in a horseshoe roll with extra shirts inside, my musette bag with a change of underwear, some cans of Red Cross food, two cans of issued beef, and five hunks of bread—food for the next five meals—my clogs, and some personal items. Under normal conditions this would have been a light load, but in my weakened condition, I entered upon the march with apprehension. I was not loath to leave Karenko, however, with the many reigns of "incidents," the hard manual labor on the farm, the reduced rations, and the overcrowded conditions.

Our ship was the *Sshozan Maru*, about thirteen hundred tons and twenty-seven years old. There were about two hundred of us in the forward hold—American, British, and Dutch officers and enlisted men—jammed in, as customary in Nipponese water movements, with a closed hold and terrific heat. Fortunately, the move northward was completed in half a day. We had to unload to a bobbing lighter where one guard fell and was comatose for a while, but none of the POWs were so unfortunate. We proceeded to a train station and were loaded on chest to back with our knees drawn up to our chins. We traveled all night without having received water since we had left Karenko. At 10:00 A.M. the next day we arrived at Tainan (Nainan). We detrained, bongoed, and were given water. Then we were trucked to camp. We had arrived at Shirakawa. The Japs had abandoned a training camp there because of insufficient water and because of a very high malarial rate. Traveling from bitter-cold Karenko to parched, burning Shirakawa in the Formosan south-central plain was quite a shock. Our months there could be summed up in a few words: hard work, short rations, brutality, constant thirst, diarrhea and malaria, dengue fever, and deaths.

Work at Shirakawa was not camouflaged by the volunteer guise. Work days were hot, blistering, and long; the work was very physical. If it had not been for the music of the British phonographs in the evening, I didn't know how we could have made it through. We listened to music such as Gigli singing "Celeste Aida"; Menuhin playing Mendelssohn's Violin Concerto; Paderewski, Chopin's Mazurka; Introduction to Act 3, Lohengrin.

Saturday, June 26, 1943. It was bright and sunny, but very depressing. Colonel Brezina died at 6:49 A.M. Of our table on board the transport coming over, the officers on my immediate right and left had gone. Frank Brezina was my cabin mate; in addition, I had known him since 1926. He served our flag in three wars (he was retired but came back because he thought he was needed) and came over here in response to a long-distance telephone request from Drake in Manila. His heart was the immediate cause of death, but a weakened condition was the basic cause.

In exactly one month after arrival here, I again had malaria. I was in the hospital for two weeks. Rumors had been flying as usual: Americans were within twenty miles of Rome, Sicily had been taken, Americans had landed on New Georgia and one other island in the Solomons, losing six cruisers, five destroyers, and twenty transports against Jap losses of one damaged cruiser, three damaged destroyers, and thirty planes. Many other POWs were beginning to be admitted with malaria.

August 15, 1943. Twenty-six years ago I received my commission as a second lieutenant. Thirty Americans received radiograms from home. I had not received either a radiogram or a letter. In two more days we would be on Taiwan a full year.

Sunday, September 5, 1943. Group Captain Rice died in the evening. He had been paralyzed and semibedfast for months. The PX sold fish flakes, canned vegetables in soy, curry powder, and AD vitamin tablets—all Red Cross items.* I weighed 64.4 kilos, about 141 pounds. I was very tired and very hungry. I got some meat shreds in the soup that night. Glately was knocked down three times; Hughes was pricked with a bayonet.

Thursday, November 25, 1943. Thanksgiving Day. On the 13th, when I was playing bridge, I had a violent stomach attack similar to those I had had the winter and spring before. It lasted about thirty minutes but left me weak and washed up. It returned and I was given soda about midnight. When it continued to be bad, Glately gave me atropine, then more soda, but it had no effect. He worked with me till 2:00 A.M., but the medicine still had no effect. After that I received several hypos which did little but eventually put me to sleep. This continued the next day and through the next night. By the following morning, my skin was a vivid yellow—definite evidence of jaundice—my urine was orange yellow and my stool, milk white. The medicos took one look at the evidence and announced that I had gallstones. I was put in the hospital, although not under any particular treatment.

A young major was in with me. Nickerson had had diarrhea since March and weighed only eighty pounds, although he seemed to be on the mend. Marshall had consumption, in my opinion, and Yankey had a bad case of stomach ulcers.

---

*One of the major reasons the POWs resisted beriberi and scurvy was the Red Cross vitamin tablets. It was suspected that much of the PX sales were of Red Cross items.—Ed.

Wednesday, December 8. Benjamin Silly died Tuesday night. He had been in the hospital several months with stomach troubles for which the Japanese were going to have him X-rayed, but never did. His sufferings were terrible. He was extremely courageous, seldom complaining and always apologetic for disturbing the rest of us. I didn't know how we all sensed the afternoon when he was going, but I noticed that the entire ward quieted down and talked in whispers. The Nipponese permitted the use of the British flag during his funeral.

Christmas morning 1943. It was as cold at Shirakawa as it had been at Karenko, but without the biting winds. Discipline was as harsh; work, even harsher. The Christmas before we had had a sort of party, playing the "Nutcracker Suite" on the gramophone. This year it was very difficult to bring back memories— we were dulled, dispirited, sitting in stupefied silence, dumb, just waiting. The year before, we still had had great hopes and expectations. It was beyond our comprehension that we would be in captivity one Christmas later. This year— we didn't know. There was no doubt in our minds as to the ultimate result, but we had almost stopped trying to figure out when the high command would give the word to go. So far, in all of 1942 and 1943, the action against Nippon had been defensive. Nevertheless, we did our best to have a Christmas Day show, and the Nipponese cooperated to the extent of giving us a nice supper with some bananas, bread and butter, and tomatoes, and we were all allowed to stay up an hour later.

On the afternoon of the 27th I developed a temperature of 101.6. I believed it to be the result of a vaccination for smallpox which we had received that morning, but Glately snorted, "Impossible." I had a chill in the evening, and the fever broke about midnight. It was recurrent malaria. Stu had the same thing.

Saturday, January 1, 1944. On my 633rd day of captivity, my fever rose to 103, and I sweated profusely. Glately put me on quinine and I felt goofy afterward. It was a horrible way to start a new year.

Wednesday, January 12, 1944. Apparently, there was a bombing attack against either the airfield near Shirakawa or some other local point. There were many loud and heavy explosions which timed about fifty seconds away—from seven to ten miles. Shepherd died in the morning. Four hundred letters came in—all British. I had not received one since captivity. Yankey was still having trouble with his ulcers and was in a bad way. I weighed 148 pounds, a gain of eight pounds while in the hospital.

Friday, February 11, 1944. Finally I was out of the hospital and was put to work at once digging a ditch. It was pick-and-shovel work serving no useful purpose, just something to keep us busy. Later we worked on concretelike soil creating a fish pond.

Tuesday, February 22, 1944. It was Washington's Birthday, the 833rd day of captivity, and a Red Letter Day—I got my first letter from home, from Mother. They permitted little of the news I wanted to hear, but at least my mother seemed well and was cheery and bright, making the statement, "All of your family are well."

Friday, March 10. There was another air raid and a new rule: total darkness. The main switch was pulled at night. We had a new low for the year, 53° F. This may not seem cold in degrees, but our thin blood, emaciated condition, heatless, drafty warehouse squad rooms, and thin clothing made it feel as cold as zero in the States. We slept in all we owned.

All too soon it was summer again, and we were subjected to scorching, blistering twelve-hour work days. With the summer came more flies, more malaria, more dysentery, and more deaths.

When the fall came, rumors of a move started again. After several days the orders came. We went through the typical crowded ride on a narrow-gauge train, this time from Nainan through Tahoku to the port of Keelung. On the night of October 9, 1944, we boarded the *Oryoka Maru* and were crowded onto the shelves in one of the holds. This was a large, round-the-world, passenger-cargo ship of the luxury-liner class. The cabins were filled with Jap civilians, women and children with their men, who were being evacuated from Malaya and the Philippines. Then we saw the picture. MacArthur was on his way back to the Philippines. He was already hitting the southern islands. As hostages, we were too exposed in Formosa so we were being rushed north. We sailed during the night of October 10. Locked in the hold, we could hear and feel the engines pounding at full speed. The ship was running fast as if it were afraid of something. Then the engines slowed and finally stopped. When we were taken on deck the next morning for our customary ten minutes of air, we were right back where we had started by the dock at Keelung. Scuttlebutt told us that the American navy was patrolling outside and had chased the ship back into the harbor. For once, and unfortunately, scuttlebutt was correct.

They tried to slip the ship out several times but without success. On October 12, again on the 13th—which just happened to be Friday—and on the 14th, we were bombed by the American Naval Air Force while locked tight in the hold of the ship tied to the dock.

We had a feeling of complete futility and helplessness while we, Americans, were on a ship that was a target for destruction by other Americans. Formations of bombers came over in waves nine times during those three days. They were using skip-bombing tactics. Many ships in the harbor were damaged, and bombs burst all around our ship, but none hit us directly.

One porthole on the side opposite the dock had been left open by accident. The officer using it gave us a blow-by-blow description of events. We thought the end had come when one bomber leveled off, came right at the ship, and released its bombs. He was late, and all his bombs passed over the ship, exploding on the dock. Many civilians and families were killed or injured. Our treatment was particularly brutal for some time after that.

During those bombings, we felt absolutely no shame or humiliation that our compatriot naval bombardiers were such lousy shots.

The ship made another run for it on October 22 and again was chased back, but during the night of the 23rd she made it. By morning she was at full speed, zigzagging toward Japan and escorted by two destroyers.

We were landed at Moji, Japan. You cannot possibly imagine our feelings when we crawled out of that hold and set foot on dry land. Two hundred fifty-nine of us had been locked in for eighteen-and-one-half days. Many days we were not allowed on deck at all.

However, it could have been much worse. On the next trip of the *Oryoku Maru* the prisoners (and Japs) were not so fortunate. Fifteen hundred American officers were being moved from Manila to Japan when she was sunk by American planes —one of the great tragedies of the war. Fewer than five hundred of them survived.

We were taken to Beppo for two weeks and were deloused and fumigated. Except for a woeful shortage of food, Beppo was a nice experience. We were billeted at hotels and fed from food stocks available to the hotel keepers. It was obvious that the Jap civilians didn't have any more food than was given to us. We had clean rooms, good treatment, quilted pallets to sleep upon, and steaming hot baths. No, the Japanese women did not scrub our backs.

Next we were moved through Moji to Pusan in Korea. We went across the channel in an old stern-wheel ferry. We were bombed again on that trip on Armistice Day, November 11, 1944, my wife's birthday. Frankly we didn't care much. We were too numb. It was freezing cold and we were acutely miserable. We had only the cotton clothes we had been wearing for almost three years, now rather threadbare. If you have been in Korea in the winter, you know how cold Pusan can be.

We were entrained in Pusan. It was another overcrowded, uncomfortable trip but there was one blessing. The train was heated and we soaked up the heat.

On that train the Japs issued wool uniforms to us, British uniforms they had brought from Singapore. Wool is better

This letter was censored by the Japs and passed through Switzerland according to our best sources. In addition, it was tested by the Germans for secret inks. Their label on the back states "High Command of the Army—Opened," and their hand stamp states "High Command of the Army—Sent." The marks of the solutions used to test for the inks can be seen on both sides of the envelope as well as all over the letter. This letter was sent May 18, 1944.

A form was enclosed by the American censor to note that he was not responsible for the streaks on the envelope or the letter.

than cotton, but it is not warm enough for bitter climates; it is also too heavy and wears one out carrying the weight around. Nevertheless, it was a vast improvement over our threadbare cotton.

We went to Mukden in Manchuria, changed trains, and were taken to Cheng Chia Tung, the last station on the railroad line. It had been a Russian military post on the eastern edge of the Gobi Desert before the Russo-Japanese War of 1904–05. We were just as far from MacArthur as they could take us.

When we detrained it was thirty-five degrees below. Centigrade or Fahrenheit? It didn't make any difference. When it got that cold, the two scales came together and it was thirty-five degrees cold. Even the mercury froze.

There in that biting cold we slowly turned blue while we had the usual roll call with the expected mistakes—the checks and double checks—before the new camp personnel satisfied themselves that we were all present and that they could sign the receipt for us to the train guards.

When the turnover finished, we were still held in ranks until we were practically stiff. Obviously, we were waiting for the customary, dramatic entry of the commandant. When finally he did appear, we were hard put to contain the mirth his ludicrous appearance created, mirth that would instantly have resulted in Jap justice—the back of the hand in the mouth.

The commandant arrived in a four-door sedan of about 1930 vintage. There was no glass in the windshield and no glass in the windows. There was no engine. The motor power was supplied by two little Manchurian ponies. The ponies were driven by a soldier in the right front seat. The car was steered, using the auto steering wheel, by another soldier in the left front seat. The commandant was almost buried under furs in the back seat. As he was slowly driven down the front of our line to inspect us, all we could see of him was a pair of magnificently waxed mustachios. He immediately became Colonel Handlebars.

That long wait in the freezing cold triggered off a high pneumonia rate within a few days. Cheng Chia Tung was our easiest camp. The old Russian barracks were warm and comfortable. Officers were no longer required to work, except for digging our own air-raid shelters. We wondered about this during the winter. In that cold there was no work we could have done. About fifteen minutes outside was as much as we could stand. But what about the coming spring?

The food was better—not good but better. We ate soy beans, millet, frozen potatoes, turnips, and parsnips. Still, there was no meat. We all gained a little weight. Just before we left Cheng Chia Tung, the Japs brought in the scales for our monthly weighing. My pre-war weight had been steady at 196. I reached Cheng Chia Tung at 118. On my last weighing there I was up to 125.

We were issued fine, warm clothing of the quilted, layer type—light in weight, but one layer on another making it very comfortable.

Bribery became easier; a lot of contraband slipped in. The guards gave us as much news as they themselves were allowed to know. Treatment was much easier. The hazing stopped. We now bowed only to officers and to sentries on duty. The Jap soldiers who knew a little English liked to sit down and try to talk to us, especially if they could cadge a cigarette.

Were the Japs seeing the handwriting on the wall? There was no doubt about it. But time went on, and during that winter of 1944 to 1945, regardless of what was happening in the south, things were relatively uneventful on the eastern Gobi. My weight again dropped to 125 pounds.

In the spring that sixth sense snapped us to alert again. This time it wasn't too hard to understand. Germany was rumored defeated, and Russia was said to be on our side. From several sources we got the persistent scuttlebutt that MacArthur had made good on his clenched-teeth statement and had returned and driven the Japs out of the Philippines. But they were rumors, just rumors.

Nevertheless, if the Russians were coming east along the Trans-Siberian Railway, then we, as hostages, were ripe as plums for the plucking. We knew that we were going to move again.

The orders soon came and we were moved back to Mukden, to Hoten compound. This was a work camp of about fifteen hundred enlisted POWs who were rotated in work groups to munition factories around Mukden. Yes, I said munition factories. A Geneva Convention violation? That's a laugh.

One advantage of Hoten was that our men worked alongside Manchurians who hated the Japs almost as much as we did. More things began to slip in. Tobacco, food, cookies, even Jap newspapers. Stu Wood and Bob Hoffman had been language students in Japan and could read the papers, so we got the news.

When the men returned from the munition factories, some would surreptitiously visit the officers' squad rooms and tell us of anything they had learned or that had happened to them.

One day it popped.

A group of men came back from a munition factory to the north. Quietly, they spread out to give us their news. The man who came to our room was almost speechless.

"Somethin's broken it, Colonel, somethin' big. The Japs are goin' nuts. They quit work in the factory and double-timed us most of the way back here. What's spooked 'em is that a Long Nose flew over the factory this mornin' and then made several passes over Mukden.* I saw it. Two or three times the bomb bays opened and a whole mess of paper fluttered down."

*The Long Nose was the B-29.—Ed.

We immediately thought of propaganda leaflets. The Japs dropped tons of them on us on Bataan. But why would Mac-Arthur be dropping propaganda leaflets at this time and over Manchuria? The soldier sputtered on. "Then, Colonel, the bomber left Mukden, flew right over the factory, and began circling about a mile to the north of us. It came down low—not more than a thousand feet I'd guess. Then some parachutes dropped with men in 'em. So help me! I saw 'em."

That staggered us.

"How many? How many were there?" I asked.

"Well, Colonel, I saw four for sure. Jonesy says that he saw at least six. I don't know. It all happened so fast."

"Was it the crew bailing out? Was the plane in trouble?"

"Not a bit of it. Naw, naw. Nothin' like that. The Long Nose circled several times more and then it dropped some more 'chutes, only this time they were bigger. Red ones and blue ones. Looked like there were boxes tied on 'em."

That sounded like equipment chutes. But why?

"You certain that plane wasn't in trouble? It didn't crack up?"

"Not a bit of it, Colonel. It circled several times more, then waggled its wings as it if were saying somethin', and then it high-tailed off south, gaining altitude fast."

We mulled that over, but we just did not know enough of what was going on to make much sense out of it.

The next afternoon there was a lot of shouting from the Jap office. Old Handlebars came out of his quarters at a half run.

A little while later, one of our yardmen sauntered through the compound. He made a motion toward the squad rooms and spoke out of the side of his mouth, "Got somethin'."

Very casually a few of us followed him into a building. When we got inside, we staked out the doors so that we would not be caught by a guard without warning. Then we told him to give. He was practically incoherent.

"Americans! Stateside Americans! In the guard room. Two
of them are Nisei Japs and they're talkin' to the guards. Talkin'
mean. Just like they was givin' 'em hell. One of 'em shook his
finger under Frisco Bobby's nose and Bobby took it—just
blinked."

Frisco Bobby was the San Francisco-reared Jap interpreter.
The yardman rushed on breathlessly. "They all have 45s
strapped to their legs and the Japs are lettin' 'em keep 'em.
And say, there's a stateside officer talkin' to Old Handlebars."

There was a lot more talk back and forth the rest of the
afternoon. I didn't remember too much detail until after dark,
when one of the colonels—I think it was Russ Ives—crawled
up a pole overlooking the commandant's quarters which were
ablaze with light. He called down in a low voice to ten or
twelve of us on the ground below him.

"There's an American officer in there, a stateside officer. He
didn't get that stomach eating Jap rice. He isn't a POW.—He's
doing the talking and Handlebars is doing the listening.—Hey,
what gives?—Old Handlebars just got up and poured some
wine in a glass for the American.—Good grief, listen to this.
The American is smoking a cigarette and he's flipping the
ashes. Get this! Get this! He just dropped the butt on the floor
and ground it out under his heel! On the floor! On the floor!"

For a long time afterward I remembered the stunned silence
that greeted this news. It was beyond our quick comprehension. We just didn't have the ability to understand it. For three
and a half POW years, we were never allowed to smoke except
when seated at a mess table and then only when we had an ash
tray within arm's length. As I have already noted, the Japs
were scared stiff of fire. Yet there was a fellow flipping ashes
all around and grinding a butt on the floor under his heel, and
Old Handlebars was watching him and taking it.

Ives went on, "Old Handlebars just went over and put on a
white kimono with big splashes of gold all over it and tied a
red obi around his middle. Wonder what that's all about?"

The man next to me gave a whistle and a half grunt. He called, "Is Colonel Wood here?"

"Right here, General."

"Stu, do the Japs wear ceremonial robes for anything other than the suicide ceremony, hara-kiri, or whatever it's called?"

"Yes, sir, on several occasions, but I don't recall any others that would fit this situation."

The general called, "Ives, does the commandant have a dagger or short sword in that red obi?"

"I don't see one, sir, but it . . ."

Just then a guard saw us and chased us into the barracks. A few moments later, a squad carrying fixed bayonets was led through the barracks by Frisco Bobby. He gave the orders. No POW would leave the squad room except to go the the *benjo*. They would register in and out of the *benjo* with a guard at the squad-room door. We hadn't had that restriction since Shirakawa. It meant something, but what?

The Japs were very uneasy that night. Usually, a patrol would pass through the barracks only once or twice a night, but that night a full squad came through every hour, checking each bed each time to see that it was occupied.

I don't think any of us slept much that night. We took stock. We had a good deal of general information as to what was going on. We knew as much as the government allowed its own people to know, but we were more familiar with the places mentioned. We could pinpoint the island hopping. We knew that the Americans were coming fast. We knew that MacArthur had cleaned up Luzon.

In addition to knowing that the Japs were getting the hell kicked out of them in the south, we knew that Germany had fallen and that the Russians were probably on our side. We knew that the Jap navy was almost zeroed out and that their air force had kamikazed itself into nonexistence. Rumor was that the Russians were coming across the Trans-Siberian railroad far—oh so far—to the north. The Russians had a lot of ignominy to revenge after the Russo-Japanese War of 1904-05. But what did all this mean to us? Just where did we stand? Suppose the emperor and the government were ready to call it a day and quit? We didn't see that it meant very much to us.

This was because we understood the Kwantung Army; the Japanese army in Manchuria was a highly efficient, thoroughly equipped, superbly trained army. They were career soldiers, trained for combat and ready, blooded by years of fighting against the Chinese. Their officers were dedicated, professional soldiers, samurai nobles, the ruling class of Japan for generations.* The Kwantung Army, we believed, would never quit, regardless of emperor or government. They would fight it out until things got bad and then would last-ditch it in the mountains of North China, north of the Great Wall.† Eventually, the men might be allowed to surrender or to take to the hills, but the officers would commit hara-kiri collectively—and just before they had their gut-slitting ceremony, they would do a mass throat slitting on us.

Admittedly, my memory was hazy about the period following the parachute drop. My day-by-day diary also was rather fragmentary. The tenseness of those moments was not conducive to thoughtful, written analysis. So I cannot say whether it was the next day or later that General Parker with the senior British and senior Dutch generals was called to the Jap office.

---

*Practically all of them were college trained, if not graduates. Many had had schooling in Europe or America. This had resulted in better, more humane treatment for the POWs than they had received on Taiwan. —Ed.

†Actually, the troops that entered Mukden had crossed the Gobi Desert by motor transport, en route from Berlin. This would make it one of the great military moves of history, and it caught the Japs unaware. They were waiting for the move down from the north when their rear was penetrated from the west, and they collapsed. The one-million-man Kwantung Army passed into captivity and was never repatriated after the war. Presumably, they all died in Siberian slave camps.—Ed.

The lieutenant generals and the governor generals had been taken to another camp months before. General King had broken his leg and was taken to the hospital, leaving General Parker as our senior.

From that meeting we learned that the Japanese emperor had asked for an armistice to discuss terms of surrender. It was not known what MacArthur was doing about this request, but the Russians had given an abrupt and definite refusal. Russia had too many memories of 1904 and 1905 and was going to fight it out until the Kwantung Army surrendered unconditionally or was destroyed. So, as far as we were concerned, we were still POWs and could expect a transfer to the mountains of North China. The generals had been told that the move would come "soon."

So there it was. Even if the Kwantung Army had decided to obey the emperor, the Russians wouldn't allow it. So where did that leave us? Right in the middle.

The generals' meeting also cleared the mystery of the parachutists. The dropped leaflets were notices of the impending armistice, printed in Japanese, Chinese, and Manchurian. Dire things were threatened if any POW were to be harmed. The men were dropped in an effort to secure our safety. The group consisted of an officer, para medics, radio operators, and American-born Japanese interpreters. Their side arms had been removed and they had become prisoners, but they had not been turned in with us. Incidentally, we later found out that not one of that group had ever stepped out of a plane before.

The general cautioned us to watch our step, to meticulously obey all rules and regulations. The Jap guards were frightened and jittery. One incident offending a scared, trigger-happy moron might set off a blazing massacre. Everything hung in a thin, delicate balance. It was a fearsome situation.

We knew that the kitchen crew had orders to keep enough meal on hand for three days' travel rations, nine hard rolls the size of a baseball for each one of us. That night at about 2 A.M.

the kitchen lights came on. That was the tip-off. We were scheduled for North China.

The next morning, as we had anticipated, we were paraded and the orders were issued. I remember that the interpreter's voice was high-pitched and quavery with excitement.

"No work details will go out until further notice. All generals and colonels will be prepared to move out on ten minutes' notice when the railroad cars come. Only what can be carried by hand will be taken with you. Three days' travel rations will be issued before departure. All other ranks will be moved later."

Things were quiet for the rest of that day, but a thousand rumors circulated. The railroad cars were on the way from Mukden. No, there would be no railroad cars. They were all up north supplying the Kwantung Army. We would be moved by truck. No, there were no trucks. We would go out on foot. The emperor had surrendered unconditionally and the war was over. The Americans had dropped a bomb the size of a grapefruit on Tokyo and it had destroyed the entire city. It was more powerful than anything the world had ever known. Rumors! Just rumors! Nothing definite came in, and since the work details did not go out there were no newspapers and no Manchurian gossip. But those rumors chased each other's tail all day.

That was the night of our scheduled concert, and General Parker thought it best if we went ahead with it to keep the POWs quiet.

That night we played several numbers, then General Parker was sent for by the Jap office. A little later some of his staff were called. We kept on playing but we didn't have our hearts in it. Then General Funk came out and motioned for me to stop the music. We were playing a number Ted Lilly had written. It's opening words were, "Home, home, I'm going home."

The general called for our attention. "All POWs will assemble at the guard gate at once. General Parker's orders. I impress upon you that this is an order—that there be no demonstration no matter what happens. I don't know what it is, but the slightest spark might set off a mess of trouble."

So there it was for us, all wrapped up and tied. We formed in dead silence. There were no "what gives? what gives?" Cold, clammy fingers were clutching our hearts right at the base of our throats. The floodlights around the gate came on. We waited. We waited. The gate swung open. Parker came out. The commandant came out. Then followed a tall, big-framed man in a uniform I did not recognize. As the matinee idol, the star, flashes across the stage, he strode dramatically to the edge of the steps. He took off his cap, and the glare from the floodlights bounced off his honey-blond hair as it would off a mirror.

He made quite a speech. At first Sergeant Hurley translated it, but toward the end the officer switched to English—flawless, except for a rather Oxford accent. His last sentences were seared in my memory and would remain there for the rest of my life.

"We of the Army of the Soviet Republics, your comrades, watched with pride and great admiration your gallant defense of the Philippines against overwhelming odds. Our hearts have gone out to you with sorrow and sympathy through the long years of your imprisonment, but tonight I burst in my heart with overwhelming feeling and great happiness to tell you, in the name of my Commanding General . . ."

The Russian shot his right arm high above his head and stood momentarily frozen in that intensely dramatic attitude.

Men rescued from drowning at the last possible minute have recalled in a few seconds their entire lives passing through their minds. As we stood there in that pin-drop dead silence, that last moment of reprieve flashed through my thoughts, not back across the three and a half years we had been waiting for this moment, hoping against hope, but forward with a surge of intense emotion which almost overwhelmed me, to a vision of the days to come—the return to my country, the rehabilitation of my mind and body, and the joyful, happy reunion with my beloved family.

The Russian's voice rose to a half shout, ". . . as of this moment, you are free."